JUST LIKE US

$\sim$

7 Ways Biblical Women Were Just Like Us (And Why It Matters)

Jennifer Hayes Yates

Author photo by Genesis Shalom Harrington

Edited by Wanda Hayes

Formatted by Jen Henderson at Wild Words Formatting.

TABLE OF CONTENTS

————— ⌒ —————

INTRODUCTION

As women we often struggle to know our place in this life. Where do we fit? What is our role? How do we balance it all?

We are constantly comparing ourselves to others, and, of course, we never think we measure up. We long to find contentment, but the world offers pleasures we ultimately turn to instead.

In our struggle to know our value, we are often told to just be ourselves, stop apologizing, and live the life we've always wanted. But deep down, we know that's not the answer.

As we seek to know our purpose, the world will keep us distracted and confused with more roles and responsibilities than we can handle. And in all of it, we just want to have peace, to feel significant, and to fulfill the purpose for which we were created.

Instead of faith, we struggle with doubt. We want truth, but we keep believing the lies of the enemy. The world surrounds us with fear and despair, but our hearts long for courage and hope.

How can we overcome the challenges to our faith in a world that is increasingly hostile to all that we believe?

I have good news!

We are not the first women to struggle with all these questions. What may sometimes seem outdated, irrelevant, and important only as literature or cool stories is actually an historical account of the lives of real people just like us. I'm talking about the Bible.

As I have studied the women of the Bible for the past year, I have learned to appreciate the truth that they were real women, just like us. They were wives and mamas and sisters and grandmas. They grappled with infertility, comparison, jealousy, and doubt. Some of them made terrible choices that led to destruction; many of them used wisdom and grace to lead others.

All of them were real women who walked this earth like you and me.

The Bible is too strange to be fiction; its characters too flawed to be made up. In fact, the more we uncover archaeological evidence, the more we verify the names, locations, dates, and way of life of these very real women whose stories are shared here.

These women's lives are testimonies of the faithfulness of God, biographies that teach us spiritual lessons, and they accurately reflect the heart of all women everywhere.

So, this collection of writings is a series of reflections on the many women of Scripture—their doubts, hopes, failures, and the lessons learned. If they could speak to us today, they would offer us the answer for all the struggles we face as women:

Just follow Jesus.

THE SEARCH FOR CONTENTMENT

IN A WORLD OF PLEASURE

FINDING FULFILLMENT:
THE WOMAN AT THE WELL

I got a complete 16-place setting of Oneida silverware for Christmas last year. I'm sure I will never serve dinner to 16 people at one time, but I was deliriously happy. I've had my eye on a new set for a while now. We have silverware we received as a wedding gift twenty-seven years ago, but our dishwasher apparently swallows forks and never gives them back.

The surviving spoons are treacherous to the tongue because they've been chewed by the garbage disposal one too many times. As happy as I am to have smooth, matching silverware, no gift on earth can fill the need in my soul to be loved, satisfied, and fulfilled.

That need is within each of us, yet we all seek to satisfy it in different ways. For the woman at the well, relationships gave her temporary pleasure, but no man could satisfy the longing of her heart.

> "When a Samaritan woman came to draw water, Jesus said to her, 'Will you give me a drink?' (His disciples had gone into the town to buy food.)

The Samaritan woman said to him, 'You are a Jew and I am a Samaritan woman. How can you ask me for a drink?' (For Jews do not associate with Samaritans.)" (John 4:7-9).

Most Jews hated Samaritans and would go out of their way to avoid them, but not Jesus. To the woman at the well, longing to be loved and fulfilled, the words of Jesus set a spark of hope in her heart:

Could this be someone who doesn't loathe me for who I am?

Jesus' reply stunned her even more:

"'If you knew the gift of God, and who it is that asks you for a drink, you would have asked him, and he would have given you living water'" (John 4:10).

She came to the well with her water jar at the noon hour when no other women would be around, probably to avoid the stares and the gossip. She came with an empty jar reflecting her empty heart, desperate for more than just liquid in a container.

And Jesus offered her Himself.

The first step in finding fulfillment is to realize that we will never find it in presents, people, or our own performance. While each of those can offer temporary pleasure, none of them can ever fill the void in our lives. Presents grow old and lose their shine; people will eventually disappoint, and our own achievements will still fall short. The only way we can be assured of a peace that passes understanding is to allow Jesus to fill the void.

Oh, I know. I doubted at first, too. How can someone I can't see or touch offer me anything I need?

> "'Sir,' the woman said, you have nothing to draw with and the well is deep. Where can you get this living water?'" (John 4:11).

I know your well of emptiness and broken promises seems far too deep for hope. But Jesus shared a secret with her that I pray you will get too.

> "Jesus answered, 'Everyone who drinks this water will be thirsty again, but whoever drinks the water I will give him will never thirst. Indeed, the water I give him will become in him a spring of water welling up to eternal life'" (John 4:13-14).

The second step to finding fulfillment in life is to understand what Jesus offers. He doesn't just promise to forgive us. What Jesus offered her, and what He offers you and me, is His very presence, filling our lives and making us complete.

The Holy Spirit is the Living Water that will fill our empty souls and satisfy every longing and desire of our hearts. We don't always recognize what we thirst for. We may seek material things, accomplishments, approval, or relationships to meet our needs. But what we really long for is God.

For our Samaritan friend, relationships with men had been her futile attempt to find love. But Jesus knew that a continual stream of men in her life would never satisfy her thirst. Only Living Water could do that. And Jesus invited her to drink.

> "He told her, 'Go, call your husband, and come back.'

'I have no husband' she replied.

Jesus said to her, 'You are right when you say you have no husband. The fact is, you have had five husbands, and the man you now have is not your husband. What you have just said is quite true'" (John 4:16-18).

In that moment, she knew there was nowhere to hide. He had just read her mail, and she was a sinful, broken woman. Surely she wasn't worthy to worship this God. But Jesus called her to come just as she was—in the right spirit and with a repentant heart.

"'Yet a time is coming and has now come when the true worshipers will worship the Father in spirit and truth, for they are the kind of worshipers the Father seeks'" (John 4:23).

Yes, you. A despised Samaritan. A lowly woman. A sinful adulterer. The Father is seeking you.

And that, my friend, is why she laid down her jar.

"Then leaving her water jar, the woman went back to the town and said to the people, 'Come, see a man who told me everything I ever did. Could this be the Christ?'" (John 4:28-29).

Oh, yes, I think you know the answer. He is the Christ, and He offers Living Water that will satisfy your soul. He knows all you have done and loves you still.

The ultimate way to find fulfillment is to lay down your empty jar. Stop trying to fill it with everything but the real thing. Come to

Jesus, confess your sins, and let Him pour out His Spirit into your life.

If you are struggling to fill the emptiness in your soul, Jesus invites you to come. Life with the Living Water is better than any gift, accomplishment, or relationship you could ever hope or wish for. He will satisfy your deepest longing, and you will never thirst again.

THE DECEPTION
OF DISCONTENT:
EVE

For me, it started with television, magazines, and social media—that feeling that I didn't quite measure up or have everything in my life that I desired. The movies showed me there was a romance and passion I felt my marriage lacked. Magazines revealed a beauty I didn't possess. Social media displayed houses and vacations I felt I could never achieve. The discontent set in.

For Eve, it started in the Garden. Suddenly, having beauty, love, and purpose in life weren't quite enough. It seemed God was holding back on her, and there was more—a wisdom and pleasure she had yet to experience.

> "Now the serpent was more crafty than any of the wild animals the LORD God had made. He said to the woman, 'Did God really say, "You must not eat from any tree in the garden?"'" (Genesis 3:1).

Eve knew God. He walked with her and Adam in the Garden (Genesis 3:8). Yet when the voice of the serpent spoke, he seemed to know what he was talking about. She bought into his lies because he told her she would be like God.

"'You will not surely die,' the serpent said to the woman. 'For God knows that when you eat of it your eyes will be opened, and you will be like God, knowing good and evil'" (Genesis 3:4).

The reality is that she was already like God—created in His image (1:26-27). But the lie Satan offered was that it wasn't quite enough, that there was more to be had outside her relationship with God. The enemy's temptation led Eve to become discontent with all God had created her to be, to enjoy, and to do. So she looked elsewhere to find the contentment she now longed for, and according to Satan, it could only be found in the one thing God had forbidden.

In our relationship with Jesus, we too have beauty, love, and purpose in life, but the enemy will often lure us to believe there is more to be had that can only be found outside our relationship with God. The temptation is to look to the world to meet our unholy desires.

It starts with doubt. "Did God really say that we shouldn't lust in our hearts? It's not hurting anyone else to fantasize about a different life."

Then we begin to distort. "Well, God wants me to be happy, so it's okay if I indulge in these extra clothes and jewelry. The Lord will provide."

And then the discontent grows. The more we begin to look for satisfaction in things other than God, the more we will crave. It's a beast that's never satisfied. But just as Eve discovered, it's a scam. What the world offers is a cheap counterfeit. Not only will the world's enticements not bring us contentment, they will eat us alive with sin, guilt, shame, and confusion.

The fruit that looked good for food was really poisonous. Eve already had a Garden full of delicious and satisfying food (1:29). Jesus reminded us in the wilderness that man doesn't live by bread alone, but by every word that comes from God (Matthew 4:4). When we seek to satisfy our cravings with anything other than God, we will be left disappointed.

That lush fruit that seemed pleasing to the eye was actually rotten and distorted. There was no beauty to be had in partaking of something God had forbidden.

When Satan attempted to make the kingdoms of the world attractive to Jesus, He responded that we should worship and serve only God (Matthew 4:10). The truth is that Jesus already owned all the kingdoms of the world and had authority over them, but He would be subject only to the Father.

When we look to the world to meet our needs, we are stating that God is not enough, that we need something outside of what He has already given us.

When Eve heard that the tree was desirable for gaining wisdom, what she didn't understand is that not all so-called wisdom is welcome. Their eyes were opened, but in a way that made them no longer innocent. They became aware of the depravity of sin.

Eve felt God was holding back something good from her, but God had already given all she needed.

When Satan tempted Jesus to throw Himself off the temple to prove He was God, Jesus let him know He had nothing to prove (Matthew 4:7). God has already proven Himself to us by sending His Son to die for us (Romans 5:8). He has not withheld anything we need, so we have no reason to test Him.

Just like Eve, we are already beautiful. We don't need more clothes, makeup, or surgeries to make us more like the image we see in the world. We need to surrender to the Holy Spirit so His beautiful fruit will bear forth in our lives (1 Peter 3:4-5).

Like Eve, we have perfect love. There is no greater love than one who would lay down his life for his friends (John 15:13). Jesus has proven His love to us in His sacrifice on the cross. He has nothing left to prove. No earthly relationship can meet all our needs and satisfy our desire to be loved. Only Jesus can do that completely.

And like Eve, we have purpose in life. Our purpose is to know God and to make Him known (John 17:26, Matthew 28:19-20). That's all the wisdom, power, and authority we need.

The next time we see a house better than ours, a spouse other than ours, or anything else the enemy whispers we need outside what He has freely given us, we can be reminded of Eve's loss of fellowship with God in the Garden.

> "Then the man and his wife heard the sound of the LORD God as he was walking in the garden in the cool of the day, and they hid from the LORD God among the trees of the garden" (Genesis 3:8).

She and Adam lost everything to gain what they thought looked better. Jesus lost His life to gain for us what is truly better.

Don't trade what God has so richly given to settle for the enemy's cheap substitute. Don't listen to the lies that pull your heart away from God. It's a scam and a trap. It looks pretty, but it's all a lie.

Find your contentment in the beauty, love, and purpose of a personal, growing relationship with God. That's all you really need to be content.

PLAYING FAVORITES: REBEKAH

————— ⟨∽⟩ —————

We like to joke about who is the favorite in my family. Well, I guess that depends upon whom you ask.

My mom (known as Mema by everyone) does an excellent job of making all four of her grandchildren believe they are her favorite. (And each of them honestly believes it. Just ask them).

Truth be told, we can be drawn toward a child with whom we have more in common. Not to mention, when there is both a son and a daughter, it is sometimes natural for mama's-boy and daddy's-girl relationships to evolve.

Those relationships can actually be beautiful and rich. But when we begin to show favoritism to one child over another, dysfunction and destruction are the end result.

> favoritism: the practice of giving unfair preferential treatment to one person or group at the expense of another[1]

No other biblical woman can testify to that pain more than Rebekah.

She had a whirlwind romance with Isaac, spent twenty years barren, and finally became pregnant with twins. When those babies began to jostle within her, she cried out to the Lord.

> "Then the LORD said to her, 'Two nations are in your womb, and two peoples from within you will be separated; one people will be stronger than the other, and the older will serve the younger'" (Genesis 25:23).

In ancient Israel, the older son received the birthright, which included the authority as head of the family and a double portion of the inheritance. But God said those roles would be reversed. Maybe right then Rebekah's heart was drawn to the younger child. Who knows? For whatever reason, as the boys grew, she began to show favoritism to Jacob.

> "The boys grew up, and Esau became a skillful hunter, a man of the open country, while Jacob was a quiet man, staying among the tents. Isaac, who had a taste for wild game, loved Esau, but Rebekah loved Jacob" (Genesis 25:27-28).

We aren't letting Isaac off the hook; he clearly favored the older son Esau who was a real man's man. But Rebekah is the object of our lesson today, because she took her affection for Jacob too far. Impulsive Esau ended up selling his birthright for a bowl of stew, demonstrating that he didn't value the promise of God (Hebrews 12:16). That birthright included the covenant promises his father Isaac had inherited from Abraham.

But when Isaac began to age and thought his life was coming to an end, he still wanted to give his blessing to Esau. The blessing, which was usually an oral statement given by the father on his deathbed, had more to do with future blessing or curse spoken over the sons (Genesis 49).

Although the birthright and blessing were usually tied together, Isaac wanted something to go to Esau since he had sold his birthright. But Rebekah overheard Isaac's wishes and made plans to deceive him.

> "Rebekah said to her son Jacob, 'Look, I overheard your father say to your brother Esau, "Bring me some game and prepare me some tasty food to eat, so that I may give you my blessing in the presence of the LORD before I die." Now, my son, listen carefully to what I tell you: Go out to the flocks and bring me two choice young goats, so I can prepare some tasty food for your father, just the way he likes it. Then take it to your father to eat, so that he may give you his blessing before he dies'" (Genesis 27:6-10).

Rebekah encouraged Jacob to deceive his father and manipulate Isaac into giving the blessing of the firstborn to him. In ancient Near Eastern law, oral statements, especially on one's deathbed, could be legally binding.[2]

Because of her favoritism and deception, Rebekah caused such division between her two sons, that Jacob had to flee for fear that Esau would kill him. Isaac and Esau were both devastated by the deception.

> "When Esau heard his father's words, he burst out with a loud and bitter cry and said to his father, 'Bless me—me too, my father!'" (Genesis 27:34).

Despite the fact that Esau wasn't completely innocent since he didn't initially value the birthright, one can't help but feel the pain in those words. How often do children cry out for the blessing of their parents? As mothers, we have the opportunity to pour out blessing on our children through unconditional love and acceptance shown through our words, our actions, and our prayers over them.

We should never show favoritism to one child over another. The damage to their hearts is overwhelming and oftentimes devastating. Rebekah had to send Jacob away because Esau wanted to kill him. Her hope was that it would be a temporary situation until Esau cooled off.

> "'When your brother is no longer angry with you and forgets what you did to him, I'll send word for you to come back from there. Why should I lose both of you in one day?'" (Genesis 27:45).

But Jacob's story was one of heartbreak, deception, and wrestling with God. When he finally returned home twenty years later and was restored to his brother, Rebekah was no longer present. Most commentators believe she had already died. She never saw her favorite son again.

Not only can our favoritism lead to damaged relationships between our children, but it will also bring pain and suffering to our own hearts. People tend to show favoritism because of some lack in their lives, some desire to find fulfillment in the love of a child.

Our fulfillment must come from our relationship with God and not our children. As mamas, we will never be perfect, but we can learn from the wisdom of the Bible, which clearly teaches us the damage caused by showing favoritism.

Rebekah's choices also put enmity between her and Isaac, which is another consequence of showing favoritism to one child. It led to her deception towards Isaac, which will always end in destruction.

Our children are different, with different personalities, temperaments, gifts, and abilities. We may have different relationships with each of them based on their uniqueness as individuals, but the love we show them should be equal.

God does not show favoritism (Acts 10:34-35, Romans 2:11, Ephesians 6:9, Colossians 3:25, 1 Timothy 5:21), and we are supposed to reflect His heart in how we love others. He doesn't play favorites, and He warns us not to either.

If you have a child that you favor for whatever reason, remember the pain caused by showing favoritism. Ask God to show you the uniqueness of each individual, and then commit to showing the same attention, affection, and affirmation to each one.

Pray words of blessing aloud over each of your children so they hear your heart for them. Look for ways to connect with each one of them. If you have shown favoritism in the past, ask God to forgive you. Make amends with any relationships that may be affected. And look to God alone for your contentment.

God can redeem our mistakes and make us into the parents He wants us to be. No relationship is without hope. So, thank God for His Word that corrects us and teaches us how to live (2 Timothy 3:16).

Lord, may we grow in our love for others so that it reflects your heart. And may our love for our children be so deeply and sincerely expressed that each of them could say without a doubt: "I'm the favorite!"

DISAPPOINTED, PROVOKED, AND MISUNDERSTOOD: HANNAH

———————— ∞ ————————

It really stinks when things in life don't go the way we expected, especially when we believe God for something in prayer but still come up empty-handed. Add to that the disillusionment that comes when others don't understand, and our sorrows only increase.

How does God expect us to deal with the disappointments, provocations, and misunderstandings in life?

As a frail human with a sinful nature, I have often reacted to the adversities of life with anger, frustration, blame, and cynicism. But God, in His grace, calls us to a higher standard.

Thankfully, we have examples in Scripture of women who have suffered as we do. The Word of God gives us a guide for every situation we find ourselves in if we are willing to study and apply the principles we find.

Hannah's story is one that gives us great hope. As we often see in ancient Israel, she was one of two wives. God intended for a man to be with one wife (Genesis 2:24), but the Israelites often followed the customs of the pagan nations around them. As you can imagine, man is not equipped to deal with more than one wife. Peninnah bore Elkanah children, but Hannah was barren, a source of both grief and shame to a woman in her day.

"He had two wives; one was called Hannah and the other Peninnah. Peninnah had children, but Hannah had none" (1 Samuel 1:2).

Every Israelite male was required to go before the Lord at the tabernacle in Shiloh three times per year. As the family went up with feasting and celebrating, Hannah only experienced grief.

"Whenever Hannah went up to the house of the LORD, her rival provoked her till she wept and would not eat" (1 Samuel 1:7b).

Every festival was a reminder of God's mercy and goodness, but to Hannah the celebration was shadowed by her failure to conceive and the taunts of wife number two. While everyone else was feasting, Hannah couldn't eat, even with Elkanah's encouragement. His love for her was great but could not sustain her in her deep grief.

So she cried out to the Lord.

"In bitterness of soul Hannah wept much and prayed to the LORD (1 Samuel 1:10).

In the midst of deep disappointment over the direction our life has taken, sometimes even the encouragement of others, while well-meaning, can't help us. Only God can. As Hannah cried out to the Lord, she began to grow bold. Rather than listening to the taunts of her rival, she decided to focus on what the Lord could do for her.

Hannah knew that only God could meet her need and help her in this situation, so she made a vow to God that if he would remember her and give her a son, she would give him back to the Lord for His glory.

> "'O LORD Almighty, if you will only look upon your servant's misery and remember me, and not forget your servant but give her a son, then I will give him to the LORD for all the days of his life...'" (1 Samuel 1:11).

Can you imagine wanting something so badly that you commit to give it away? But think of Hannah's heart! Her desire to have a son was so she could bring glory to her God. When Hannah got her mind off herself and focused on the kingdom, she was able to commit her life completely to the Lord.

She began to see that even our children are in God's hands. Of course, to no longer be barren would remove her shame and sadness, but having a son would no longer be about her. It would be about her service to God. Hannah vowed to God that if He gave her a son, she would commit him to a life of service to the Lord, not at age 25 which was the custom for Levites, but "all the days of his life" (11).

Can we commit to God to serve Him all the days of our lives, even when life doesn't go as we had planned?

As Hannah continued to pray, the priest observed her lips moving and thought she was drunk. He rebuked her based on this observation. Once again misunderstood and criticized, Hannah could have given up all hope. But rather than getting upset or walking away, Hannah calmly replied.

> "'I am a woman who is deeply troubled. I have not been drinking wine or beer; I was pouring out my soul to the LORD'" (1 Samuel 1:15b).

Hannah had grown stronger through her time in prayer. Though misunderstood, she continued to believe God to hear and answer her. There will always be those who don't understand our hearts or our passion for the Lord, but in those times if we continue to pursue Him, we will have peace.

> "Eli answered, 'Go in peace, and may the God of Israel grant you what you have asked of him'" (1 Samuel 1:17).

Hannah walked away from that encounter with peace, a new appetite, and a new attitude.

> "Then she went her way and ate something, and her face was no longer downcast" (1 Samuel 1:18b).

God answered Hannah's prayer and gave her a son; Hannah kept her word and gave him back to God. When he was weaned (usually around the age of three), she took him to the house of the Lord to live and serve there with the priest. Now, you may be thinking, "How is that a happy ending? Surely she felt as much grief from giving her child away as she did from being barren!"

But what follows in the Word is the prayer Hannah prayed when she left her little boy with the Lord.

"My heart rejoices in the LORD; in the LORD my horn is lifted high. My mouth boasts over my enemies, for I delight in your deliverance. There is no one holy like the LORD; there is no one besides you; there is no Rock like our God" (1 Samuel 2:1a-2).

Hannah's joy was complete not in the birth of her son but in the blessing of her God. She had come to realize that in the midst of her disappointment, pain, and brokenness, what her heart really needed was Him. Hannah needed to know He was with her. She needed to know that when others were against her, God was for her. Hannah needed the confirmation that when others misunderstood her, God knew her.

Beloved, God is with you. He is for you. And He knows you. Whatever you are struggling with today, cry out to the Lord, commit your life to Him no matter what, and trust that He will work all things together for your good (Romans 8:28).

Ask Jesus to draw your eyes to Him and not your troubles. Let His love be enough to sustain you. There is no god like our God. He is enough.

CHEATING ON GOD: GOMER

───────⌒⌒───────

I made a promise to the Lord recently that I would not check my phone until after my morning quiet time with Him. I did it because I got up one day and clicked on the weather to see if I wanted to go on the back porch. Then I clicked on a message I saw from a friend. Next, I tapped the Facebook app because I remembered it was a friend's birthday, and I wanted to share my birthday wishes before I forgot.

Thirty minutes later, I realized I had not even thought about Jesus.

So, I repented and turned to my Bible to begin my time with Him. But it wasn't quite the same. Already, my heart and mind had been filled with all the hurry and happenings of the day. That sweet connection I usually start my day with seemed to have slipped away.

Oh, for a heart that just seeks the Lord! I so want Him to be the number one priority of my day. Not just because it makes me better; I want Him to know that I treasure our relationship above all else in my life. I want to show Him that through my actions.

Yet, so often my heart is quickly turned aside to the things of the world, the cravings of sin, the lust of the eyes, the boasting of what I have and what I do (1 John 2:16).

When I allow the world to take priority over the God who rescued me, it's spiritual adultery. Unfaithfulness. I'm basically cheating on God.

That's what God told the Israelites. He called the prophet Hosea during a time of spiritual apostasy. Hosea lived during the final days of the Northern Kingdom of Israel. Because of the unfaithfulness of God's people, He allowed them to fall to the Assyrian Empire in 722 B.C. but not before He sent many prophets to warn them and urge them to repent.

"When the LORD began to speak through Hosea, the LORD said to him, 'Go, take for yourself an adulterous wife and children of unfaithfulness, because the land is guilty of the vilest adultery in departing from the LORD'" (Hosea 1:2).

We may think that directive was pretty harsh, but God had called the Israelite nation to be a people set apart unto Him. He rescued them from slavery in Egypt, brought them into a land flowing with milk and honey, gave them victory over their enemies, and promised that the Messiah would come through them to save the world.

For Israel to be God's people, they had to worship Him alone. He called them to faithfulness. Yet, they had rejected His rule over them in asking for kings. They had rejected His Law by doing what was right in their own eyes. And they had spurned His love by worshiping false gods.

God spoke to the people through Hosea, calling them back from their unfaithfulness. He used Hosea's family life as an example of His relationship with Israel.

> "Hear the word of the LORD, you Israelites, because the LORD has a charge to bring against you who live in the land: 'There is no faithfulness, no love, no acknowledgment of God in the land'" (Hosea 4:1a).

Yet, in His love and covenant faithfulness to Israel, God's rebuke was to bring about their reform. God still wanted their hearts!

> "The LORD said to me, 'Go, show your love to your wife again, though she is loved by another and is an adulteress. Love her as the LORD loves the Israelites, though they turn to other gods...'" (Hosea 3:1).

See, Gomer had left Hosea and their three children and apparently ended up in slavery. So Hosea had to buy her back, even though she was his wife. We, too, have been marred by sin and bound in slavery to it. But Jesus paid the price to redeem us from that life and purchase us as His very own.

> "For you know that it was not with perishable things such as silver or gold that you were redeemed from the empty way of life handed down to you from your forefathers, but with the precious blood of Christ, a lamb without blemish or defect" (1 Peter 1:18-19).

Just as God showed His heart for Israel by instructing Hosea to buy back his wife, He has shown His love for us in sending Jesus to save us from our sins. We love Him because He first loved us (1

John 4:19). And He demonstrated that love to us in a tangible, visible form—His Son (Romans 5:8).

Just as Gomer was loved and brought back home to her family, God has called us out of the world of sin and brought us into the kingdom of the Son He loves, in whom we have redemption and the forgiveness of our sins (Colossians 1:13).

So what made Gomer stray from her family?

Gomer wasn't content with the family God had given her. The temptation of the world, the lust of the flesh, the pride of life—all led to her downfall into a life of slavery, separated from those who loved her.

But God. He loved her too much to leave her there. He still sought her. He still loved her. He still wanted her love and obedience.

When our hearts are led astray, God will still pursue us. He loves us as we are, but as Max Lucado once said, He loves us too much to leave us there. He will continue to rebuke, correct, and discipline us in order to draw us back to Him (2 Timothy 3:16). And as much as we hate discipline, we can take heart in the fact that, just like a good Father, He disciplines those He loves.

> "No discipline seems pleasant at the time, but painful. Later on, however, it produces a harvest of righteousness and peace for those who have been trained by it" (Hebrews 12:11).

I'm sure Gomer paid a high price for her adultery. Sin will always cost more than we think. Thank God, if we turn back to Him, He is waiting with open arms for us to come home.

So, maybe checking my phone before my quiet time doesn't seem like a big deal. Maybe it's not. But for me personally, it can easily become an idol, something that steals time, mindfulness, and devotion away from my time with God. If we truly want to love the Lord with all our hearts, souls, minds, and strength, then we had better guard against those things that would lead our hearts away from Him.

> "Sow for yourselves righteousness, reap the fruit of unfailing love, and break up your unplowed ground: for it is time to seek the LORD, until he comes and showers righteousness on you" (Hosea 10:12).

God has done everything in Christ to make a way for us to know Him. Let's don't cheat on Him by making anything else a higher priority.

He's God. He deserves to be first.

THE CHAOS OF COMPARISON: MARTHA

Have you ever been passionate about serving God, but then got caught up in the chaos of comparison?

Sometimes our intentions can be so well-placed, yet our execution becomes distracted, muddled, and tainted with our own jealousies and comparisons to what we think somebody else is or is not doing.

It's a tactic of the enemy, for sure; yet one that we so easily fall prey to. Rather than focusing on the Lord and serving Him with the gifts and talents He's given us, we get distracted, upset, and resentful over how someone else chooses to serve.

> "As Jesus and his disciples were on their way, he came to a village where a woman named Martha opened her home to him. She had a sister called Mary, who sat at the Lord's feet listening to what he said. But Martha was distracted by all the preparations that had to be made" (Luke 10:38-40a).

Martha was probably the older sister, since she is listed first and she opened her home to Him. She had a gift for hospitality—for not only providing a place for Jesus to come and rest and hang out with friends, but also preparing a savory meal for Him.

Martha was a servant. Her heart was drawn to service, provision, creating a space of warmth, welcoming, and hospitality for Jesus. But when she realized Mary was just sitting at His feet, not offering to help, she became upset.

> "She came to him and asked, 'Lord, don't you care that my sister has left me to do the work by myself? Tell her to help me!'" (Luke 10:40b).

Before we judge her too harshly, how many times have we said the same thing? How often have we looked around at those who just warm the pews and don't want to help serve at church? How many times have we judged those around us who seem content to sit at His feet but don't have a desire to get their hands dirty, to get outside the doors of the church and meet the needs of those around us?

If we are honest, we have all wanted to run to Jesus, crying, "Tell them to help!"

Jesus' response to Martha is interesting, because I feel like He was okay with her act of service. I think He appreciated all Martha's hard work and her efforts to serve Him in that way. But His gentle rebuke had more to do with helping Martha see that she had allowed her heart to become distracted from what was really important.

> "'Martha, Martha,' the Lord answered, 'you are worried and upset about many things, but only one thing is needed. Mary has chosen what is better, and it will not be taken from her'" (Luke 10:41-42).

32

Mary had chosen what is better—not because sitting at His feet is the only thing needed. That doesn't fit the context of the rest of the New Testament's teaching on service (Matthew 25:35-40, 1 Peter 4:9-11, for example). She had chosen what is better because her heart was wholly focused on the Lord. She wasn't distracted with comparison and worry over what someone else was doing.

Granted, we all must prioritize time with God. Our service will be useless if we are not first spending time in His presence and growing in Him. But the one thing needed is our whole hearts surrendered to Jesus. And that requires devotion that is not distracted by comparison.

God has given us great diversity in our giftings on purpose. Some of us are drawn more toward discipleship—learning and teaching. Some are more naturally bent toward service—giving and helping. God will use us in the ways He called us, but it's not our place to judge or worry about how someone else is serving.

"We have different gifts according to the grace given us. If a man's gift is prophesying, let him use it in proportion to his faith. If it is serving, let him serve; if it is teaching, let him teach; if it is encouraging, let him encourage; if it is contributing to the needs of others, let him give generously; if it is leadership, let him govern diligently; if it is showing mercy, let him do it cheerfully" (Romans 12:6-8).

When our focus is on Jesus, it won't matter how others serve or don't serve. With eyes on our Savior, we will be passionate for the things He has called us to do. Mary and Martha both had a close friendship with Jesus. When their brother Lazarus died, Martha was the first to run out to greet Jesus. She expressed her complete faith in Him.

> "Jesus said to her, 'I am the resurrection and the life. He who believes in me will live, even though he dies; and whoever lives and believes in me will never die. Do you believe this?'
>
> 'Yes, Lord' she told him, 'I believe that you are the Christ, the Son of God, who was to come into the world.'
>
> And after she had said this, she went back and called her sister Mary aside. 'The teacher is here,' she said, 'and is asking for you'" (John 11:25-28).

Martha's declaration of faith in Jesus is one of the most profound statements of belief in the New Testament, much like Peter's statement of faith in Jesus as the Messiah (Matthew 16:16). And her heart for her sister is seen as she tenderly tells her "He's asking for you."

When our focus is on who Jesus is and how we can best serve Him, God will use us in unimaginable ways. Let's stop worrying about those who don't appear to be serving Him, and let's just do our best to serve well.

We are all one in Christ, so we bless Him most when we serve Him together as one body—called, anointed, diversified, yet unified for the glory of God.

REJOICING WITH OTHERS: ELIZABETH

Jealousy. Envy. Competition.

We can sometimes get so caught up in comparing ourselves to others, that we find it difficult to celebrate their successes. If someone else experiences a joy (or even a sorrow) that overshadows ours, we find ourselves upset that their joy (or pain) seems more important than our own.

God has given us each other so that we can share our struggles, hopes, fears, and joys with one another. When we allow our focus to be on ourselves, however, we miss out on the blessing of true friendship.

Elizabeth was the wife of Zechariah, a priest. She was barren and well past child-bearing years when the story begins. At the time, no prophet had spoken in Israel in 400 years. The people were under Roman occupation and waiting for the Word of God to be fulfilled, for the Messiah to come and save them.

The angel Gabriel appeared to Zechariah, announcing the birth of a son to his wife, Elizabeth. This son would be named John, and he would go before the Lord to prepare the people.

"Many of the people of Israel will he bring back to the Lord their God. And he will go on before the Lord, in the spirit and power of Elijah, to turn the hearts of the fathers to their children and the disobedient to the wisdom of the righteous—to make ready a people prepared for the Lord" (Luke 1:16-17).

Can you imagine what Elizabeth must have felt when she realized she really was having a baby in her old age? Her husband was so astounded by the news that his disbelief caused the angel to render him mute until the birth! Elizabeth, however, was overjoyed that the Lord had blessed her in such a way.

"After this his wife Elizabeth became pregnant and for five months remained in seclusion. 'The Lord has done this for me,' she said. 'In these days he has shown his favor and taken away my disgrace among the people'" (Luke 1:24-25).

The *NIV Study Bible* text note says this about her seclusion:

"In joy, devotion and gratitude that the Lord had taken away her childlessness."[3]

Elizabeth spent five months rejoicing with Zechariah over what God had done. She didn't go to the market and tell everyone that she was finally having a baby, that God had removed her disgrace. She didn't post a cute picture of her baby bump on Instagram. She rejoiced only with God and her husband for what God alone had done.

But then Mary, her relative, had a visit from Gabriel, too. She also would have a Child, but He would be the Son of God.

"So the holy one to be born will be called the Son of God. Even Elizabeth your relative is going to have a child in her old age, and she who was said to be barren is in her sixth month. For nothing is impossible with God" (Luke 1:35b-37).

So, when Elizabeth was six months pregnant, after keeping all that God had done in her life to herself, Mary showed up with news of her own.

"At that time Mary got ready and hurried to a town in the hill country of Judea, where she entered Zechariah's home and greeted Elizabeth. When Elizabeth heard Mary's greeting, the baby leaped in her womb, and Elizabeth was filled with the Holy Spirit" (Luke 1:39-41).

Elizabeth had no idea what was going on prior to Mary's arrival. She hadn't received a text that Mary was on the way. She knew only that her own child was special. She knew he would "be a joy and delight" and that many would "rejoice because of his birth" (1:14). The angel had prepared Zechariah and Elizabeth with news that their child would be "great in the sight of the Lord" and "filled with the Holy Spirit even from birth" (1:15).

But none of that knowledge caused Elizabeth to miss what was happening in Mary's life. When that baby leaped in her womb, she was empowered by the Holy Spirit to declare what God was doing through Mary.

"In a loud voice she exclaimed: 'Blessed are you among women and blessed is the child you will bear! But why am I so favored, that the mother of my Lord should come to me?'" (Luke 1:42-43).

I love that she got loud! Her heart was completely focused on what God was doing in and through her friend. I'm sure she was dying to share her own news. I mean, after all, barrenness was cause for shame and dishonor in their culture. She was experiencing her own miracle.

But Elizabeth was filled with the Spirit of God. And she was overjoyed for Mary. It was Mary's moment to shine.

> "'As soon as the sound of your greeting reached my ears, the baby in my womb leaped for joy. Blessed is she who has believed that what the Lord has said to her will be accomplished'" (Luke 1:44-45).

Oh, that our hearts would be so focused on what God is doing in the lives of those around us that we wouldn't become upset when someone else is getting the spotlight!

Sometimes we are hurting, but someone else needs our comfort. At times we are winning, but someone else needs to be celebrated. It takes real Christian maturity to focus on others' needs when we have needs of our own. But that's what trusting God is all about.

> "Rejoice with those who rejoice; mourn with those who mourn. Live in harmony with one another" (Romans 12:15-16a).

I love this next part of the story:

> "Mary stayed with Elizabeth for about three months and then returned home" (Luke 1:56).

Seriously, Luke?? You couldn't give us a few more details?

Remember, Elizabeth was six months when Mary arrived, so apparently she stayed until the birth of John. I imagine Elizabeth shared with her all that God had done. I'm sure they enjoyed many days of conversation, sharing their hopes, fears, and joys to come.

That's what true friendship between mature Christians looks like: selflessness, humility, building each other up; rather than jealousy, envy, and competing for attention.

May the Holy Spirit empower us to focus outward, not seeking attention of our own, but making much of others. May we be so in tune with the Lord that we are attentive to needs around us, encouraging, rejoicing, and comforting others as needed.

In doing so, God will also meet our needs and send the encouragement and comfort we need, even if it only comes from Him. He is Immanuel, God with us. And He makes much of us.

THE SEARCH FOR VALUE

IN A WORLD OF PLENTY

JESUS AND THE
VALUE OF WOMEN

———————— ⟪∽⟫ ————————

I recently shared a message with some ladies at a conference based on what I learned from Captain Marvel. I know—that sounds ridiculous, but it has been one of the most impactful messages I have shared.

The movie is available on dvd if you missed it on the big screen. (If you have kids, I recommend reading some Christian reviews before you decide if it's appropriate for them.) I loved it, and I want to share some of those thoughts with you from the story.

When the Captain Marvel movie first came out, there was a lot of buzz about it being a feminist movie. In fact, the lead actress, Brie Larson, made the comment that they expected it to be the "biggest feminist movie of all time."[4]

I have to admit, I had a little trepidation about the movie beforehand simply because of her statement. I didn't want Captain Marvel to be political; I just wanted to enjoy the movie.

The comic book character Captain Marvel arrived in the late 60s, right on the heels of one of the feminist movements in America. She is a powerful female super-hero. The character has been through several transformations over the years, but it is no surprise

43

that Disney chose to tell her origin story now—as the feminist movement is seeing a re-surge in momentum.

Captain Marvel is a story of redemption, sacrifice, and protecting the innocent. It's also a story of self-discovery and breaking out of boundaries placed by others. Rather than feeling put off by some political agenda, I felt myself cheering her on as I watched her bullied by those who didn't think she could measure up in roles traditionally assigned to men.

So, I asked myself, "Why?"

Why has there been this surge of feminism in recent years? Why do women feel the need to be empowered, especially in a first-world country where we already have so many rights and freedoms?

Why this need?

Women want validation, approval, significance, and empowerment, and they are willing to fight for it. So, I really began to pray and think about why women feel this way. And I was reminded of a few things.

My daddy left us when I was twelve. I will admit: I was left feeling neglected and rejected. I struggled with insecurity for years. Then I think of all the women I know who have been abused, neglected, or mistreated. Their pain and suffering are very real.

Yet within the church, we mostly avoid the idea of feminism because of its secular nature. Most of the feminist agenda today is focused on sexual freedom, the right to choose a career over an unborn child, or belittling men and viewing them as inferior in an effort to regain the respect women think they deserve.

I get it. Many women have not gotten the jobs they deserved or equal pay (although, to be fair, there are many factors that affect that outcome besides gender). Lots of women have been objectified and mistreated by men. But the world's message that we overcome by independence, knowing our own power, and trusting in ourselves is not the answer.

How do we respond?

Rather than hiding from or disavowing these issues, the church needs to address the needs of women with grace and truth. Too often, we react with knee-jerk opposition, instead of addressing the issues with biblical application.

Some responses from "Christian" circles have been blog posts and books which encourage women to just stand up for ourselves, finding our purpose and identity in self; but we will never be empowered by depending on our own weak, sinful flesh.

Rather, let's look to Scripture to define who we are as women and what that means for our significance and value.

In the Old Testament, women were highly valued members in a patriarchal society. They participated in worship and community (Psalm 68:25, 1 Samuel 1) including public reading of Scripture (Deuteronomy 29:11, 31:12), established businesses (Proverbs 31), held leadership roles (Judges 4:4), and did manual labor (Ruth 2:7). Women were listened to by men (2 Kings 22:14-20) and considered a blessing (Proverbs 18:22, 19:14).

By the time Jesus came on the scene, much of that had changed. Because of the influence of Greek and Roman culture and the sin nature of all people, women had been excluded from worship except for the women's court. They were not allowed to even touch the Scriptures.

According to the traditions of the religious leaders (man-made laws), it was a disgrace for a man to be seen talking to a woman in public. Men could divorce women for any reason, but women did not have the same standard. Women were little more than servants, considered on the same level as criminals. Their testimony was not even considered valid in court.[5]

Then Jesus came on the scene and turned their cultural expectations upside down.

Jesus validated women. He treated them as He treated all people—with love and respect. He gave women approval, significance, and spiritual power that the men and religious leaders deemed inappropriate. He spoke to women, offering healing, forgiveness, restoration, approval, and comfort.

Indeed, Jesus went to the cross, not just for men, but also for the women whom society deemed of less significance than animals. And therein lies our value. We are all unworthy—man, woman, and child alike—yet Jesus has validated our worth with His very life.

Yes, the need for women to feel validated and significant is very real—just as it is for everyone. But we don't have to fight the status quo to have our needs met, nor do we have to hide our face in the sand and pretend these needs don't exist. We need only turn to Jesus.

JESUS VALIDATED WOMEN: THE WOMAN CAUGHT IN ADULTERY

———————— ⌒⌒ ————————

Have you ever been in a situation in which you were treated differently because you are a woman—looked down on, unjustly criticized, or demeaned? Maybe you were abandoned, objectified, or just a pawn in someone else's game.

In an era in which women were considered as low as criminals, on the same level with animals in some cases, Jesus turned social expectations upside down. He didn't come to abolish the Law but to fulfill it, giving the full understanding—the spirit that was intended—behind the law.

In doing so, Jesus revealed that the heart of God towards women was vastly different from the ideology of the Roman and Jewish culture of His day. One of the best examples of His validation of women can be seen in the account of the woman caught in adultery.

> "But Jesus went to the Mount of Olives. At dawn he appeared again in the temple courts, where all the people gathered around him, and he sat down to teach them. The teachers of the law and the Pharisees brought in a woman caught in

adultery. They made her stand before the group and said to Jesus, 'Teacher, this woman was caught in the act of adultery. In the Law Moses commanded us to stone such women. Now what do you say?' They were using this question as a trap, in order to have a basis for accusing him" (John 8:1-6a).

First, these leaders were in a battle with Jesus. They weren't offended with the woman—she didn't mean that much. In fact, they weren't offended with the sin either, because adultery requires two people, and the man was nowhere to be found. Their offense was with the One whom all the people had gathered around, thus threatening their power and authority.

Second, they twisted the law in order to trap Jesus. Yes, there were laws that called for death as the punishment. The Old Testament law was given in order to show us the righteous standard of God. The punishment was often severe in order to deter breaking the law. God knows the power of evil to corrupt those around it.

The laws these leaders referenced, however, called for the death of both parties for adultery (Leviticus 20:10, Deuteronomy 22:22). They weren't interested in justice, only in trapping Jesus. If He had agreed with them, it would have put Him at odds with the Roman government, who forbade the Jews' carrying out executions. If He had not agreed with them, He would have been going against the Mosaic Law.

And third, the religious leaders saw the woman as simply an instrument in their dispute with Jesus. An accusation of this type required eyewitness testimony, so you can imagine her shame. Then they brought her to Jesus when a crowd was gathered, humiliating her even further. They didn't bring the man out; but, after all, she was just a woman.

Jesus cared little for their confrontation, but He cared much for her. Since Jesus knows everyone's heart, He had the ability to see her for who she was. And He put a stop to their cruel game.

"But Jesus bent down and started to write on the ground with his finger. When they kept on questioning him, he straightened up and said to them, 'If any of you is without sin, let him be the first to throw a stone at her.' Again he stooped down and wrote on the ground.

At this, those who heard began to go away one at a time, the older ones first, until only Jesus was left, with the woman still standing there. Jesus straightened up and asked her, 'Woman, where are they? Has no one condemned you?'

'No one, sir,' she said.

'Then neither do I condemn you,' Jesus declared. 'Go now and leave your life of sin'" (John 8:6b-11).

I can't think of anything more validating than to have God call out your enemies in front of you. Jesus wasn't going to play their game. His heart was for her. He saw her shame and humiliation, and He knew her sin was no worse than theirs. In a culture that saw her as nothing more than a pawn in their game, He saw her as a valued person in need of mercy, forgiveness, compassion, and restoration.

"Jesus' words had the effect of shifting the attention from himself and the woman to the accusers. Conscience began to do its work. Their age made them leaders, and their longer experience of sin gave them greater cause for self-accusation. Only two remained—the sinner and the Friend of sinners."[6]

Jesus didn't condone her sin. But He didn't condemn her either. You know what He did? He saw her. He didn't overlook her or demean her or treat her as a second-class citizen. He saw her as a highly-valued child of God. And that's what drew her heart to Him in repentance.

Her sin was wrong, but so was their cruelty toward her. Jesus would stand for neither. He sent them away, dropping their stones to the ground. He sent her away, dropping her past behind her.

No matter what we have done, the price for our sin has been satisfied in Jesus. He calls us to follow Him, leaving the past, the shame, and the humiliation behind and walking with Him in the power of His Spirit.

So, if you have ever been mistreated because you are a woman, you can rest in the calm assurance that you are highly valuable to the heart of God—so much so that He sent His only Son to pay the price for your sin. You can trust God to right every wrong, so let go of any offense done to you. And you can put your rocks down, too.

JESUS SHOWED APPROVAL TO WOMEN: THE WOMAN WHO ANOINTED JESUS

————— ᴄᴏ —————

She walked slowly into the room, knowing she wasn't invited, knowing she didn't belong, knowing she was probably about to be cast out—yet her desire to show her love to Jesus spurred her on.

She had heard Him preach and realized the depth of her sin. After all, a woman such as herself—who had given her body to so many men out of desperation—could not possibly expect to find love and acceptance from God. Yet His message told her just that—she was loved!

That knowledge had so filled her with joy and peace as she surrendered her heart to Him, that she couldn't hold back any longer. She had to show her love in return, the only way she knew how. And all she had to give was an alabaster jar of perfume. And her devotion.

But the religious leaders would have nothing to do with her kind. To them, she was just a dirty, low-down, sinful woman. What would they do? What would they think? And how would Jesus respond?

She believed He was truly God—no one else could speak with such authority and love at the same time. No one else could convict her of sin by His words, yet comfort her with the offer of love and forgiveness. And so, she risked the rebuke, the rejection, and the embarrassment for the chance to show her love in return.

I am always so amazed at the way Jesus responded to women. The outcasts of society, they were often considered on the level of criminals in Roman and Jewish culture at that time. Yet, Jesus treated women on equal footing with men, created in His image, worthy of love and respect.

"Now one of the Pharisees invited Jesus to have dinner with him, so he went to the Pharisee's house and reclined at the table. When a woman who had lived a sinful life in that town learned that Jesus was eating at the Pharisee's house, she brought an alabaster jar of perfume, and as she stood behind him at his feet weeping, she began to wet his feet with her tears. Then she wiped them with her hair, kissed them and poured perfume on them" (Luke 7:36-38).

Now to us, washing Jesus' feet with her tears, drying them with her hair, and pouring perfume on them sounds a little strange. Apparently, the Pharisee disapproved as well.

"When the Pharisee who had invited him saw this, he said to himself, 'If this man were a prophet, he would know who is touching him and what kind of woman she is—that she is a sinner'" (Luke 7:39).

Her acts of devotion and gratitude to Jesus were overlooked by the Pharisee. Instead, he saw only what she represented to him—a sinner and everything unclean. What the religious leader had failed to understand is that we are all sinners, including him.

53

"Jesus answered him, 'Simon, I have something to tell you.'

'Tell me, teacher,' he said.

'Two men owed money to a certain moneylender. One owed him five hundred denarii, and the other fifty. Neither of them had the money to pay him back, so he canceled the debts of both. Now which of them will love him more?'

Simon replied, 'I suppose the one who had the bigger debt canceled.'

'You have judged correctly,' Jesus said" (Luke 7:40-43).

I love how patient Jesus was with the Pharisee. He was teaching him a lesson about sin, love, and forgiveness. And also about the worth of every person.

"Then he turned toward the woman and said to Simon, 'Do you see this woman? I came into your house. You did not give me any water for my feet, but she wet my feet with her tears and wiped them with her hair. You did not give me a kiss, but this woman, from the time I entered, has not stopped kissing my feet. Therefore, I tell you, her many sins have been forgiven—for she loved much. But he who has been forgiven little loves little'" (Luke 7:44-47).

You see, her actions were not lewd at all, as the Pharisee might have judged. Instead, she was showing the hospitality that Simon should have shown Jesus as a guest in his house.

Jesus looked at her and saw someone who loved much because she had been forgiven much. It didn't matter if she was woman, man, or child; it didn't matter if she was rich or poor; it didn't matter if she was black or white; it didn't matter if she was a princess or a prostitute—she was loved by God and forgiven of her sins.

"Then Jesus said to her, 'Your sins are forgiven.'

The other guests began to say among themselves, 'Who is this who even forgives sins?'

Jesus said to the woman, 'Your faith has saved you; go in peace'" (Luke 7:48-50).

Only God has the ability to see a person's heart. And He sees each of us as sinners in need of His saving grace. None of us are beyond His reach. Nothing we have done is too bad. We are all undeserving of His love and mercy. *All of us.* Yet He values us all just the same.

Jesus' gentle rebuke of the Pharisee in front of the "sinful" woman is a reminder to us all that Jesus showed approval to women in a culture that denied them respect and value.

Maybe you have been disrespected and undervalued because you are a woman. Remember that God created us all in His image and loves us equally. His forgiveness and grace are offered to all.

May Jesus' words bring you comfort and peace today as you look to Him alone for your worth.

HIDDEN IDOLS OF MY HEART: RACHEL

———————— ⟨∞⟩ ————————

I have a very unhealthy relationship with food. I know...if you know me personally, you will be one of those people who say, "I don't know why you're always worried about your weight. You're so little."

What they don't know is the pain of my childhood, growing up overweight and being teased because of it; being overlooked, left out, unfriended, and unnoticed; and how easily I can gain because of my petite frame.

What they fail to realize is that it's not always my current weight that is the issue; it's the fear of gaining it back that keeps me bound. As much as I love Jesus and know that I am made in His image, I still to this very minute struggle with my weight. I am constantly dieting, thinking about food, wanting to indulge, feeling guilty when I do, upset over every pound gained, and hating myself when I can't control it.

It's the hidden idol in my life. And as much as I hate typing these words through my tears that blur the screen, I am coming clean today. I'm sure that someone else out there is struggling with a hidden idol, something that has a hold of their minds, their time, and their attention, other than God, and they can't seem to let it go.

Remember how Jacob worked seven years because of his love for Rachel? When Rachel's father deceived him into marrying Leah, he worked another seven years for Laban (Genesis 29). Eventually, Jacob tired of working for Laban and sought to take his family and return to his own relatives. God had been with Jacob and blessed him with much livestock, so he told Leah and Rachel that God was calling him back to his native land (Genesis 31).

"Then Rachel and Leah replied, 'Do we still have any share in the inheritance of our father's estate? Does he not regard us as foreigners? Not only has he sold us, but he has used up what was paid for us. Surely all the wealth that God took away from our father belongs to us and our children. So do whatever God has told you'" (Genesis 31:14-16).

So Jacob gathered together his family and livestock and fled from Laban. Only, Rachel stole her father's household gods. After three days, Laban caught up with them and confronted Jacob. Jacob had no idea the gods were among his belongings, so he allowed Laban to search their tents, declaring death to anyone who had them.

"Now Rachel had taken the household gods and put them inside her camel's saddle and was sitting on them. Laban searched through everything in the tent but found nothing" (Genesis 31:34).

We don't really know why Rachel took her father's gods. Maybe she thought she deserved something from her father. Perhaps she thought they would bring her protection or comfort. Maybe she wanted to get back at her father for giving her sister to Jacob first. Or perhaps they were fertility gods that she thought would help her have a child.

> "When Rachel saw that she was not bearing Jacob any children, she became jealous of her sister, so she said to Jacob, 'Give me children, or I'll die!'" (Genesis 30:1).

Rachel was filled with jealousy and obsessed with having a child to the point of desperation. When we become obsessed about anything other than God, we have opened ourselves up to the seduction of idols we think will bring us comfort or peace.

In any case, Rachel clung to the objects of her past, even as she was being led into the Promised Land with Jacob. What can we learn from Rachel's hidden idols?

First, they caused her to lie. She kept their presence from her husband and hid them from her father. Idols will do that. Our shame and embarrassment will cause us to hide our longings from those we love.

Second, they were powerless. These idols that had gripped her heart were in reality so small, she could sit on them! She risked her life to hide something that had no power to save her. We too will hold tightly to something we think will bring us satisfaction, when in fact it is powerless to give us the peace, satisfaction, or fulfillment we think we are missing.

Third, they separated her from God. After Jacob finally wrestled with God face to face, he led his family to Bethel to worship.

"So Jacob said to his household and to all who were with him, 'Get rid of the foreign gods you have with you, and purify yourselves and change your clothes. Then come, let us go up to Bethel, where I will build an altar to God, who answered me in the day of my distress and who has been with me wherever I have gone'" (Genesis 35:2-3).

We can't worship God with all our hearts if we're holding onto our hidden idols. We have to let go of those things that draw our hearts away from complete trust in Him. I can't obsess about food and body image and appearances and still be fully devoted to God. Because when I do, I am saying that God is not enough. I am placing my insecurities in my own hands instead of His. I am emphasizing my ability to control my circumstances instead of trusting in His ability to care for me.

This is hard, y'all. Because I have controlled my appetite and eating habits for over thirty years. And I have done it out of fear. I always told myself it was because I wanted to be healthy, and I do. I want to be able to serve God as long as I can and be a good steward of this temple He came to dwell in.

But the older I get, the harder my weight is to control, and suddenly I find myself considering diet pills and extreme measures to keep the weight off. That's when I know it's a problem. Like Rachel, I've become desperate to maintain control of my destiny. She wanted a son, but even when she got one, she wasn't satisfied.

"She became pregnant and gave birth to a son and said, 'God has taken away my disgrace.' She named him Joseph, and said, 'May the LORD add to me another son'" (Genesis 30:23-24).

That's what our false gods do—they make us crave more of what doesn't have the power to satisfy us in the first place. They blind us to the truth of what we do have. They keep us serving them out of fear. And when we do achieve what we are desperate for, we begin to enjoy the feeling of control and power over our circumstances. And that's a dangerous place to be.

Ironically, the one thing Rachel was so desperate for is what killed her. She died giving birth to her second son (35:18). Jacob may have gotten the idols out of his household, but Rachel never let go of the hidden idol in her heart.

To be completely honest, I haven't either. But I know that I can't hold onto my obsession to be thin and still worship God with all my heart. So, today, I'm laying down my idol. I don't have to be controlled by my fears and insecurities, and neither do you. After all, God has a work for us to do building His kingdom on earth.

We need undivided hearts, set free to fear only Him, seeking and serving Him without the distraction of a little god with no power.

"Teach me your way, O LORD, and I will walk in your truth; give me an undivided heart that I may fear your name" (Psalm 86:11).

What holds your heart in its grip? What keeps you bound in fear or desperate for control? What do you think about, talk about, and worry about most of all? Don't bow to the image you have created in your mind. Ask God to release you from anything you are desperate for besides Him.

"'Love the Lord your God with all your heart and with all your soul and with all your mind and with all your strength'" (Mark 12:30).

God wants all our love. And He deserves it.

OVERCOMING THE STING OF REJECTION: LEAH

---- ⚬ ----

Rejected. Ignored. Refused. Not too many things sting quite like the pain of rejection. To feel that something about us is not good enough hurts, especially when there is the added pain of comparison.

Besides Jesus Himself, I don't think anyone in the Bible suffered the pain of rejection quite like Leah. My heart always aches for her.

The oldest daughter in her family, she should have been the first married off, but her younger sister Rachel caught the eye of Jacob because she was "lovely in form, and beautiful" (Genesis 29:17).

Leah, on the other hand, had "weak eyes" (17). The Hebrew word translated *weak* in this verse can mean "soft, delicate, gentle, or tender."[7]

Commentators, therefore, differ on what this description actually means, from weary and dull to light blue eyes in a race of dark-eyed beauties. In Hebrew culture, bright eyes were admired. Leah's weak eyes would have been considered a defect.

The bottom line is that she was not wanted by Jacob because of her looks. For any woman, that is painful to bear. For her father, it was too much to bear. So although Laban had promised Rachel to Jacob in exchange for seven years of work, after the wedding feast, he deceitfully sent Leah in to lie with Jacob instead, marrying off his oldest daughter first according to custom.

When Jacob awoke and saw that he had been tricked, he was furious:

> "'What is this you have done to me? I served you for Rachel, didn't I? Why have you deceived me?'" (Genesis 29:25b).

So, Laban agreed to give Rachel to him also in exchange for seven more years of labor. Because of his love for Rachel, Jacob agreed. But he didn't love Leah.

> "Jacob lay with Rachel also, and he loved Rachel more than Leah…" (Genesis 29:30a).

Leah was tolerated but not chosen. Have you ever felt that way? Maybe a painful divorce left you feeling unwanted, a job promotion didn't go your way, or a friend left you out of her group.

At first Leah became desperate for Jacob's love and attention, and sometimes we do that, too. God opened her womb because he saw that she was hated (31). As she began to bear children for Jacob, she clung to the hope that with each son, she would win Jacob's affection.

She called the first son Reuben "'because the LORD has seen my misery. Surely my husband will love me now'" (32). She called the second son Simeon because "'the LORD heard that I am not loved, he gave me this one too'" (33). The third son she named Levi because she said, "'Now at last my husband will be attached to me, because I have borne him three sons'" (34).

With the birth of every son, Leah hoped that Jacob would love her. But at some point, she realized that it wasn't Jacob's love she ultimately needed. Leah finally came to the realization that the love and approval of God was what really mattered in her life.

"She conceived again, and when she gave birth to a son she said, 'This time I will praise the LORD'" (35a).

No more desperation for Jacob, no more feeling hated by him—just praising the Lord. Leah saw what we need to see: all the striving in the world for love and acceptance won't fulfill us—only God can do that. When we change our focus from the people we are trying to please to the God we want to please, He fills us with joy and peace that can't be gained elsewhere.

Even though her own sister became jealous and they continued to battle over Jacob and child-bearing, Leah continued to find her joy in the Lord, and His favor was on her. She looked to God to bless her and cause her to be honored from that point on. And He did. The promise to Abraham, Isaac, and Jacob of the coming Messiah who would bless the whole world with salvation was fulfilled not through Rachel, but through Leah.

God saw the heart of the one rejected and unloved, and He chose her.

"For he chose us in him before the creation of the world to be holy and blameless in his sight" (Ephesians 1:4).

"For we know, brothers loved by God, that he has chosen you, because our gospel came to you not simply with words, but also with power, with the Holy Spirit and with deep conviction" (1 Thessalonians 1:4-5).

You, beloved, are chosen too. You are not tolerated. You are cherished by your heavenly Father. Accept it. It matters not what you see in the mirror, how you feel on your worst day, or what anyone else thinks of you.

You are chosen to know Him, to love Him, and to serve Him. So refocus your heart and mind away from the desperate strivings for acceptance and approval and toward the praise and glory of the Lord. When you understand the compassionate heart of your Father, you will want to know and serve Him more. And that is why you were chosen.

"'You did not choose me, but I chose you and appointed you to go and bear fruit—fruit that will last'" (John 15:16).

We were chosen by the King of all creation. Instead of wasting time nursing the sting of rejection, we are free to bear fruit with joy and praise. Like Jesus, who bore the deepest pain of rejection ever, let's turn our eyes to heaven and walk in the authority and anointing of the calling of God on our lives.

"Therefore, as God's chosen people, holy and dearly loved, clothes yourselves with compassion, kindness, humility, gentleness, and patience. Bear with each other and forgive whatever grievances you may have against one another. Forgive as the Lord forgave you. And over all these virtues put on love, which binds them all together in perfect unity" (Colossians 3:12-14).

Let's forgive those who hurt us, who make us feel less-than, and let's set our hearts on serving God and praising Him.

After all, He didn't choose us for nothing.

WOMEN WHO FIND THEIR BEAUTY IN CHRIST

—————————— ⚮ ——————————

What do you think is beautiful to God? We women concern ourselves quite a bit with beauty, don't we? I think Jesus is into beauty, too!

We are spending the day camping with some friends, and what an absolutely beautiful day this has been! We went for a run by the lake, and I couldn't help but marvel at the beauty all around. A heron swooped down and lighted near the bank as a gentle breeze floated past us. The sway of the trees, the warmth of the sun, and the deep blue of the sky were all reminders that our Creator has the monopoly on beauty.

If you are anything like me, I am deeply moved by beautiful things. I love to surround myself with colors—pillows, throws, candles, artwork—anything that makes me smile.

I think Jesus is moved by beauty, too. Ecclesiastes 3:11a says "He has made everything beautiful in its time…." You know what I believe God takes and makes most beautiful? An ugly, sinful heart that surrenders to Him.

We spend so much time trying to be beautiful, feel beautiful, and look beautiful. In a world where *selfie* is actually a word, our culture is obsessed with what we see in the mirror (or camera.) And then we come to a verse like this one:

> "Your beauty should not come from outward adornment, such as braided hair and the wearing of gold jewelry and fine clothes. Instead, it should be that of your inner self, the unfading beauty of a gentle and quiet spirit, which is of great worth in God's sight" (1 Peter 3:3-4).

I used to be intimidated by this verse, because I thought, "With my propensity for talking, I surely don't have a gentle or quiet spirit!" But then I realized two things about this verse.

First, it says a quiet spirit, not a quiet person. My talkative nature is the personality God gave me, and He can use it for His glory. I now see a quiet spirit as the opposite of an unruly spirit. It's not about whether I talk a lot or not; it's about whether I submit my spirit (and mouth) to God or not. When we are surrendered to the Holy Spirit, His Spirit is working through us to reveal His beauty to those around us.

Second, He doesn't care if we braid our hair or wear gold jewelry. He just says that's not where our beauty should come from. What if we spent as much time seeking to make our inner selves beautiful through His Spirit, as we spend trying to make our outer selves beautiful?

So how do we do that?

> "Rather, clothe yourself with the Lord Jesus Christ, and do not think about how to gratify the desires of the sinful nature" (Romans 13:14).

In other words, spend more time with Jesus and you will be beautiful! That's the beauty that makes Jesus smile. And He is the Author of everything beautiful!

So the next time you look in the mirror and fret over what you see, remember to let Jesus make you beautiful from within. His beauty in you is all the world needs to see. Who knew it was that easy or inexpensive to get a makeover?

YOU ARE NOT FORGOTTEN: HAGAR

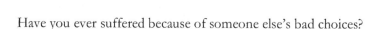

Have you ever suffered because of someone else's bad choices?

It's bad enough when we suffer the consequences of our own failures, but when we have to pay the price for someone else's sin, it's hard not to grow bitter. Maybe your spouse was unfaithful, a child was rebellious, an employer cheated you, or a church member abused you.

The suffering we endure at the hands of others can cause us to retaliate in anger or turn away from God altogether. We may become so afraid of being hurt again, that we begin to make choices not in line with God's Word.

And at times we may feel totally unseen, unheard, and forgotten by God. Hagar must surely have known how that felt. An Egyptian slave to Abraham and Sarah, Hagar was the pawn used to try to make God's promise come to pass.

You see, Abraham had been promised by God that he would be the father of many nations and that through him all the world would be blessed. But he was an old man, and Sarah was barren (Genesis 15:1-6). After ten years of waiting for God's promise to materialize, Sarah did what many of us would do—she took matters in her own hands.

> "Now Sarai, Abram's wife, had borne him no children. But she had an Egyptian maidservant named Hagar; so she said to Abram, 'The LORD has kept me from having children. Go, sleep with my maidservant; perhaps I can build a family through her'" (Genesis 16:1-2).

In Abraham and Sarah's culture, having a male heir wasn't just convenient—it was essential for having any stake in society. Knowing that many Assyrian and Babylonian customs allowed for a servant to be a surrogate, Sarah suggested allowing her slave, Hagar, to sleep with her husband in hopes of her becoming pregnant and giving them the child they were waiting for.

The problem is that wasn't God's plan or in keeping with His promise. In her impatience with God's timing, Sarah looked for a solution of her own. Hagar just got caught in the middle. When Hagar did become pregnant, she began to despise her mistress (Genesis 16:4b). Now, I'm not sure what kind of relationship they had to begin with, but I feel in my woman-ness that they were friends, even though Hagar was a slave.

In all their travels away from home to a foreign land, I imagine having another woman around to talk to would have forged a relationship between the two of them. And besides, Sarah was allowing Hagar to sleep with her husband. She must have felt at least some measure of trust in her.

But Hagar began to feel proud. She forgot her place as a slave and began to make Sarah feel bad for not being able to get pregnant. In the midst of this drama, Hagar became prideful. And we've done it, too. We've been hurt and confused, and instead of running to God, we've grown angry, prideful, or bitter.

So Sarah blamed and complained to Abraham.

> "'You are responsible for the wrong I am suffering. I put my servant in your arms, and now that she knows she is pregnant, she despises me'" (Genesis 16:5).

Abraham didn't stand up for Hagar in the least (He did have to live with Sarah), and he let Sarah do what she wanted with Hagar. So Sarah began to mistreat her (Genesis 16:6). Having been used and abused, and knowing what awaited her when this child would be born, Hagar ran away.

Have you ever felt like just running away from those who have mistreated you? Perhaps you still bear a painful reminder of the wrong done to you, and you just don't know how to deal with it anymore. Maybe you feel a little like Hagar.

In the wilderness of her wandering, God was there. He met her right where she was and made her think about where she had been and where she was going (Genesis 16:7-8).

> "Then the angel of the LORD told her, 'Go back to your mistress and submit to her.' The angel added, 'I will so increase your descendants that they will be too numerous to count'" (Genesis 16:9-10).

He sent her back to submit to Sarah because there was no life for Hagar and her child except through repentance and surrender.

Hagar may have been outside God's plan, but she was not outside His love.

Even when we struggle with the wrongs done to us to the point of walking outside His will, He still loves us. Though this illegitimate child was not the child of the promise to Abraham, God was still with him and promised to bless him, because He heard of her misery.

> "She gave this name to the LORD who spoke to her: 'You are the God who sees me,' for she said, 'I have now seen the One who sees me'" (Genesis 16:13).

You are not forgotten. God hears you. God sees you. God promises you.

Even when we fail, even when we don't get it right, He still hears our cries of misery. He still sees our pain. And He still has a promise for us. All we have to do is turn back and surrender.

Hagar's story didn't end there. Her son Ishmael, which means "God hears," grew and became antagonistic toward Isaac, the son of the promise (Genesis 21:8-9). Ishmael knew that although he was the firstborn, he wasn't the true heir.

In Sarah's ongoing jealousy, she encouraged Abraham to get rid of Hagar and Ishmael (Genesis 21:10). Since she had her own son, she no longer needed to hold onto the mess she had made. So God assured Abraham he would care for them (Genesis 21:11-13). Hagar and Ishmael were sent away, but they were never outside God's love, protection, or provision.

"God heard the boy crying, and the angel of God called to Hagar from heaven and said to her, 'What is the matter, Hagar? Do not be afraid; God has heard the boy crying as he lies there. Lift the boy up and take him by the hand, for I will make him into a great nation'" (Genesis 21:17-18).

Ishmael grew and became an archer, married a woman from Egypt (Hagar's home country), and went on to become a nation, just as God had promised (Genesis 21:20-21).

No matter the wrong that was done to you, you have a choice in how you respond. You can allow the bitterness to keep you outside the will of God, or you can turn back to God and submit to His authority.

He hears you. He sees you. He has not forgotten you.

God still loves you and He still has a promise for you.

Will you trust Him with it?

THE SEARCH FOR PURPOSE

IN A WORLD OF CONFUSION

WOMEN WHO
FOLLOWED JESUS

———————— ⟨∞⟩ ————————

"Follow your heart!" the world cries.

"Follow your dreams!" they insist.

In a culture that encourages self-discovery, self-expression, and defining our own meaning in life, it's easy to get caught up in the hype and illusion that we can best create our own world of our own making.

The problem with this philosophy is that it doesn't work for all people. Sure, some can succeed in the world's eyes by sheer determination and work ethic. But in reality, our hearts are deceptive and our dreams are not always within our reach.

"The heart is deceitful above all things and beyond cure. Who can understand it?" (Jeremiah 17:9).

Often what our hearts desire is not what is best for us. And many outcomes in life are simply beyond our control. Jesus called twelve apostles to follow Him. They had jobs, families, maybe even dreams, but they laid it all down to follow Jesus.

"'Come, follow me,' Jesus said, 'and I will make you fishers of men.' At once they left their nets and followed him" (Matthew 4:19-20).

We sometimes forget that many others followed Him as well, including women. I often wonder what that looked like. What did they give up to follow Him? Why were they willing to? How did they serve Him?

The Greek word for *follow* means "to follow; accompany; to follow or be a disciple of a leader's teaching."[8]

The call to follow demands a commitment.

"Then Jesus said to his disciples, 'If anyone would come after me, he must deny himself and take up his cross and follow me'" (Matthew 16:24).

When some told Jesus they would follow Him but made excuses about putting if off until later, Jesus had this response:

"'No one who puts his hand to the plow and looks back is fit for service in the kingdom of God'" (Luke 9:62).

Jesus said we would have to deny ourselves and take up our cross. He told His followers to count the cost before they came (Luke 14:25-35). Many people said they wanted to follow Him because they saw the miracles and benefits. But Jesus warned them that the cost would be high.

The world's call to forge our own path sounds great compared to the high cost of following Jesus. But when we seek our own way, we will still find obstacles and circumstances over which we have no control. Pain and suffering have no purpose or remedy within our self-made world.

The truth is that we will face suffering in this life either way—the difference is that when we follow Jesus, we have the Prince of Peace in our hearts—the One who has overcome the world and its suffering (John 16:33).

The call to follow demands obedience.

> "'When he has brought out all his own, he goes on ahead of them, and his sheep follow him because they know his voice'" (John 10:4).

If we want to follow Jesus, we have to know His voice through His Word. To follow Jesus means we follow His teaching. We can't be followers if we are ignorant of what we are following.

> "'My sheep listen to my voice; I know them, and they follow me'" (John 10:27).

We must spend time with Jesus through the Word, not just reading but studying, meditating, and hiding His Word in our hearts. And we must remember that He told His followers that if they loved Him, they would obey Him (John 14:15).

Our culture dictates putting our own desires ahead of anything else so that we can follow our dreams and be the person we want to be. But Christ calls us to lay down our desires to follow Him into a "new and living way" (Hebrews 10:20). As followers of Christ, we seek Him daily through prayer, worship, submission, and obedience to His Word.

The call to follow demands service.

> "'Whoever serves me must follow me; and where I am, my servant also will be. My Father will honor the one who serves me'" (John 12:26).

When I read about the women who followed Jesus, I often wonder what they did. How did they serve Him?

> "In Galilee these women had followed him and cared for his needs. Many other women who had come up with him to Jerusalem were also there" (Mark 15:41).

I think about Martha preparing meals and Mary who sat at His feet (Luke 10:38-42). I think they give us such an amazing example of the broad context of service.

> "After this, Jesus traveled about from one town and village to another, proclaiming the good news of the kingdom of God. The Twelve were with him, and also some women who had been cured of evil spirits and diseases.... These women were helping to support them out of their own means" (Luke 8:1-3).

Don't you love these little snapshots into the lives of these women?

We don't know exactly what they did, but we can piece together that they followed Jesus and His disciples, they were under His teaching, they ministered to His needs, and they supported His ministry financially.

They were an active part of the ministry as followers of Christ. They made a decision to leave behind their own plans and dreams to follow Him. They gave up their time, their own will and way, to follow the Master.

They ministered to others and met financial needs of the ministry because they believed in the One who saved them and delivered them from sin. Their focus changed from seeking their own desires to meeting the needs of the Savior.

After Jesus ascended to the Father, these women were there with the other disciples, waiting for the Holy Spirit whom Jesus had promised.

> "They all joined together constantly in prayer, along with the women and Mary the mother of Jesus, and with his brothers" (Acts 1:14).

Their decision to follow Jesus didn't diminish who they were. The call to follow Him was a call to self-sacrifice, but it was the answer to the problem we all have: We can't in our own sinful nature become who we think we want to be. Our hearts will lead us astray; our dreams will often be unattainable at worst and disappointing at best.

The call to follow brings life.

The call to follow Jesus is the call to be the women God created us to be, to follow a higher calling of serving the Creator of the universe, to fulfill His plans for us, and to live the life that brings glory to Him.

JUST LIKE US

It's the call to serve something outside ourselves, something better than the best version of ourselves, Someone who holds the world in His hands and knows the plans He has for us.

And they are plans for our ultimate good—a good that doesn't expire when we breathe our last, but an eternity that far outweighs any advantage we think we have in living for self. Why would we give up the dreams of our own making to follow Christ? I can't answer for anyone else. I don't know what was in the hearts of the women who followed Him on this earth. All I know is what He did for me.

> "This is how God showed his love among us: He sent his one and only Son into the world that we might live through him. This is love: not that we loved God, but that he loved us and sent his Son as an atoning sacrifice for our sins" (1 John 4:9-10).

God validated my worth when He sent His Son to die for me. His sacrifice made a way for me to know the Creator of the universe and live my life with a higher purpose. Because of Him, I will live forever, and how I live on this earth matters in a way that is beyond me.

Following Jesus isn't easy. Sometimes the cost seems so high and the way too difficult. The cost was high and the way difficult for Him, too. But He endured it because of His love for you and me.

> "Let us fix our eyes on Jesus, the author and perfecter of our faith, who for the joy set before him endured the cross, scorning its shame, and sat down at the right hand of the throne of God" (Hebrews 12:2).

The joy before Him was our redemption—that's why He endured such suffering. But on the other side of that cross was victory when He rose on the third day, defeating sin, hell, and the grave. In Him, we have that victory, too!

Because of His great love for you, Jesus has given His life that you might know Him. Spend time at His feet, abide in His Word, and fellowship with others who are following Him. The rewards far outweigh the cost.

Because nothing else we give our lives to can make an eternal difference in our world than being women who follow Jesus.

WOMEN ON MISSION
WITH JESUS

———— ∞ ————

In a culture that was often dismissive and seldom encouraging to women, these ladies who followed Jesus took their place alongside the men, valued in the eyes of Jesus, respected, validated, and encouraged in their devotion to Him.

They supported His ministry out of their own means, attended to His needs, and stayed at His side as Jesus endured the torture of the cross. In every gospel account, the women are identified at the cross and at the tomb.

I can only imagine how long the Sabbath seemed, as they waited in physical rest but surely emotional unease for the dawn of Sunday. Several different women are identified at the tomb that day throughout the gospel accounts, each of them longing to be by His side and care for His body.

> "After the Sabbath, at dawn on the first day of the week, Mary Magdalene and the other Mary went to look at the tomb. There was a violent earthquake, for an angel of the Lord came down from heaven and, going to the tomb, rolled back the stone and sat on it. His appearance was like lightning, and his

THE SEARCH FOR PURPOSE IN A WORLD OF CONFUSION

clothes were white as snow. The guards were so afraid of him that they shook and became like dead men" (Matthew 28:1-4).

We know from Mark's gospel that the women were there to anoint Jesus' body with spices. They set out while it was still dark and arrived at the tomb just at dawn only to find the stone rolled away and an angel there, the soldiers passed out cold.

> "The angel said to the women, 'Do not be afraid, for I know that you are looking for Jesus, who was crucified. He is not here; he has risen, just as he said. Come and see the place where he lay. Then go quickly and tell his disciples: "He has risen from the dead and is going ahead of you into Galilee. There you will see him." Now I have told you'" (Matthew 28:5-7).

Come and see the place where he lay. Come close. Look for yourselves. See the evidence. He is not here. His Word is true. Now go and tell.

These were the women who had chosen to take up their cross and follow Him. These were the women who weren't afraid to stay at the cross when others fled. These were the women who devoted themselves to serving Jesus. And these were the women He entrusted to carry the good news to others.

I have often said that being on mission with Jesus is all about coming and going. We come into the secret place with Him in worship, prayer, and Bible study. We come in and close the door and sit with Him and feed on His Word.

Then we open the door and go out into the world to share the love and truth and grace that He has shown us. When Jesus touches and changes our lives, we can't help but want to tell others what He has done for us.

Imagine how His mother Mary's life was changed—a virgin, betrothed to Joseph, scandalized by pregnancy, yet entrusted to raise up the Son of God in her home. Mary Magdalene, possessed by not one, but seven demons, then set free by the power and compassion of the Lord.

Joanna, wife of Chuza, the manager of Herod's household; Salome, wife of Zebedee and mother of James and John; the woman at the well; the woman caught in adultery; the woman with the issue of blood; Mary and Martha—so many women whose lives were changed by the Savior.

Jesus defied the cultural influences that dismissed women to the level of second-class citizens. According to their man-made rules, women were not allowed to touch the Torah, to worship in the temple (only in the women's court), or to speak to a man in public.

They weren't considered worth educating, and their testimony was not considered valid. Yet Jesus chose to reveal His resurrection first to women, sending them to testify to the others.

Where Eve once stood in a garden, defying the command of God and taking on the consequences of that disobedience, Mary Magdalene now stood in another garden and received the redemption of Jesus—not only saved but now commissioned to go and bear fruit.

"Jesus said, 'Do not hold on to me, for I have not yet returned to the Father. Go instead to my brothers and tell them, "I am returning to my Father and your Father, to my God and your God"" (John 20:17).

Jesus could have first revealed Himself to Peter, James, or John. If the entire gospel is a cleverly fabricated story, the writers surely would have designed a narrative that conformed to the cultural expectations of the day.

But they didn't and it isn't.

Instead what we read is the astonishing detail and remarkable account of Jesus revealing the true heart of God for women, the role He created us for when we were made in His image and commissioned to be fruitful and multiply.

In Jesus' revelation to the women at the tomb, we see redemption, restoration, and a reversal of the stain of sin in the first garden.

"In him we have redemption, the forgiveness of sins, in accordance with the riches of God's grace that he lavished on us with all wisdom and understanding" (Ephesians 1:7).

We were not created to overpower or usurp the role of men. We were created to serve alongside them in carrying the gospel to the world.

"So the women hurried away from the tomb, afraid yet filled with joy, and ran to tell his disciples. Suddenly Jesus met them. 'Greetings,' he said. They came to him, clasped his feet and worshiped him. Then Jesus said to them, 'Do not be afraid. Go and tell my brothers to go to Galilee; there they will see me'" (Matthew 28:8-10).

My sister in Christ, don't be afraid to come and go. Come close and worship Him. You are not second rate in Jesus' eyes. Then go and tell. You've been empowered by the One who reigns over all.

WOMEN WHO CHOOSE THE BETTER THING: MARY OF BETHANY

———————— ✸ ————————

Do you have a consistent daily quiet time with Jesus? That used to be a real struggle for me, but once I began to seek regular time with the Lord, my life drastically changed. My marriage improved, my relationships grew, and I began to experience real joy and peace in my life. That's what having a relationship with Jesus is all about.

When I first gave my life to Jesus as a college student, I would spend hours in the evenings on the floor of my room, studying the Bible, praying, and listening to Christian music. For the first time in my life, I felt as if I had real purpose and acceptance. I treasured that time I spent each evening at His feet.

Then I graduated, started teaching, and got married (all in the same year!), and life got incredibly busy. All of a sudden I had people other than Jesus who wanted my time and attention. The distractions left me anxious and upset, and my time with Jesus became less and less. I wanted to be with Him, but I struggled to find the time for Him.

"As Jesus and his disciples were on their way, he came to a village where a woman named Martha opened her home to him" (Luke 10:38).

Do you ever have really good intentions to spend time with Jesus, but then get so distracted that you can't even hear what He's saying? I feel for Martha. She invited the Savior to her house for a good reason: She wanted to spend time with Him, serve Him, and worship Him.

But then again, hosting Jesus and the disciples would have been no small task. I don't know how big her house was or if all her dishes were clean, but I would have a hard time feeding thirteen men at my house right now. All of a sudden, Martha's mental state went from seeking Jesus to seeking a plan.

Some of you are smiling right now because you can't even count how many times your prayer list turned into a to-do list. Or how many times you planned to get up early to seek Him, but your kids decided to get up early too.

"She had a sister called Mary who sat at the Lord's feet listening to what he said. But Martha was distracted by all the preparations that had to be made. She came to him and asked, 'Lord, don't you care that my sister has left me to do the work by myself?'" (Luke 10:39-40).

(I love this part.)

"'Tell her to help me!'" (Luke 10:40b).

Yep. That's what happens. We end up cranky and irritable and taking it out on everyone around us. I've been there. The problem is that we are really upset with ourselves, because we know that deep down it's just a matter of priorities. We all have the same twenty-four hours in a day, and we all make our own schedules.

Granted, at different seasons of life, our days can look totally different. Parenting small children may require seeking Him in the middle of nap time. Or in the middle of the night. Caring for a sick family member may mean that our time with the Lord is at a different time every day. I've been there, too. But no matter the time or the season, we can choose the better thing.

> "'Martha, Martha,' the Lord answered, 'you are worried and upset about many things, but only one thing is needed. Mary has chosen what is better, and it will not be taken away from her'" (Luke 10:41-42).

I love the Lord's tender response to Martha. I can almost see Him patting the floor next to Mary, offering Martha a place at His feet. Because that is the place where, at least for a moment, schedules and baths and laundry take a brief backseat. Oh, I know they are important, but they find a way of all coming together in just the right manner at His feet.

Are you worried and upset about many things, finding yourself distracted and maybe even bitter at those who seem to have it all together? Hear the Lord's tender invitation to you. Leave the dishes in the sink and come away with Him for a little bit. You will find yourself longing for more of Him, and that which we long for, we will find time for.

If you need a daily devotional to get you started in the Word, check out *Drawing Ever Closer: 365 Days of Transformational Truth.*

Only one thing is needed. This is your purpose. Choose the better thing.

WOMEN WHO WORSHIP: HANNAH, MARY, DEBORAH, AND MIRIAM

-------- ⟨∽⟩ --------

My daughter-in-law visited Israel last year, the one thing at the top of my bucket list. As you can imagine, we were eager to hear about her trip when she came home. So, we met them at a restaurant and listened as she shared stories from her adventure.

Moriah told us about experiencing the actual places Jesus visited when He was baptized in the Jordan, shared the Sermon on the Mount, and prayed at Gethsemane.

Then with tears in her eyes, she said something I'll never forget. Moriah told us that although it was really cool to walk where Jesus walked, the most touching and memorable experience for her was worshiping with other believers from all over the world.

She experienced that "wow" moment with the realization that Christ came to indwell believers. His presence is no longer just in the temple. His presence is within each of us, wherever we are. For her, the opportunity to lift her voice to God together with other believers was the most touching part of her journey. And so it should be. After all, that's what we were made for.

The Bible gives us many examples of women who worship, but for the sake of brevity, I just want to share three characteristics we can find in them.

Women who worship are focused on God and not themselves. Two examples of this that stand out to me are Hannah and Mary. Both of them had similar songs of praise in response to what God had done in their lives.

Hannah had been barren, but God gave her the child she prayed for. After weaning the boy, she took him to the temple and dedicated his life to the Lord. There she erupted in praise to God, but her focus was not on her son or herself. Her focus was on her God.

> "'There is no one holy like the LORD; there is no one besides you; there is no Rock like our God'" (1 Samuel 2:2).

Likewise, Mary, who had been betrothed but not yet married, received news that she would be with child and that He would be the "Son of the Most High." Most of us would have fallen apart at such news, but Mary responded with worship.

> "And Mary said, 'My soul glorifies the Lord and my spirit rejoices in God my Savior, for he has been mindful of the humble state of his servant. From now on all generations will call me blessed, for the Mighty One has done great things for me—holy is his name'" (Luke 1:46-49).

At first glance, we may think Mary is focused on herself, but remember that she had been given news that could have led to her death under the law. Her focus here is not on herself, but on her God whom she trusted.

She went on to sing:

> "'His mercy extends to those who fear him, from generation to generation. He has performed mighty deeds with his arm; he has scattered those who are proud in their inmost thoughts. He has brought down rulers from their thrones but has lifted up the humble'" (Luke 1:50-52).

Mary gave all her praise to God, who fills "the hungry with good things" (53). Women who worship aren't self-absorbed and focused on themselves—their looks, their stuff, their entertainment, their own needs. They keep their eyes on the Kingdom and worship God for who He is.

Women who worship aren't concerned with what others think. Deborah was a woman before her time—a wife, prophetess, judge, and warrior all in one. She was so confident in leadership that her commander wouldn't even go into battle without her (Judges 4:8).

When the battle was over and their enemies had been defeated, Deborah didn't hold back from praising her God, no matter who was listening.

> "'Hear this, you kings! Listen, you rulers! I will sing to the LORD, I will sing; I will make music to the LORD, the God of Israel'" (Judges 5:3).

Deborah went on to recount all the God had done on behalf of His people. In a culture and time in which women were not usually respected or followed, Deborah was one who commanded respect because of her confidence in God.

She listened to the Lord and followed Him; that's why people, including men, were willing to follow her leadership. She wasn't ashamed of her God. She was surrendered to Him; therefore, she didn't worry about what others thought of her worship.

Her praise was for God alone.

Women who worship set an example for others. In Exodus when God led His people out of Egypt and through the Red Sea on dry ground, Moses and the Israelites came out praising God on the other side. Then Miriam picked up a tambourine and led the women in praise.

> "Then Miriam the prophetess, Aaron's sister, took a tambourine in her hand, and all the women followed her, with tambourines and dancing. Miriam sang to them: 'Sing to the LORD, for he is highly exalted. The horse and its rider he has hurled into the sea'" (Exodus 15:20-21).

Miriam didn't just follow Moses in worship—she led the women in worship as well. Our worship is always a witness to others. And worship is much more than music and singing. Remember the woman with the alabaster jar? She poured out her worship on Jesus at great cost to herself.

She had lived a sinful life and was most likely looked down upon by society. But when she heard Jesus was at the Pharisee's house, she had the courage to show up uninvited.

"When a woman who had lived a sinful life in that town learned that Jesus was eating at the Pharisee's house, she brought an alabaster jar of perfume, and as she stood behind him at his feet weeping, she began to wet his feet with her tears. Then she wiped them with her hair, kissed them and poured perfume on them" (Luke 7:37-38).

Don't you think she knew that the pious religious leaders were going to berate her for even showing up, much less demonstrating such an extravagant outpouring of love and devotion?

"When the Pharisee who had invited him saw this, he said to himself, 'If this man were a prophet, he would know who is touching him and what kind of woman she is—that she is a sinner'" (Luke 7:39).

Jesus knew what was in his heart, and rather than rebuking the sinful woman, he rebuked the Pharisee. The leader had not shown the normal acts of hospitality for Jews in that day—washing the feet of the guests, greeting with a kiss, or providing oil for His head. But she had. Because she came focused on Jesus, not caring what anyone else thought, she set an example of true worship for all those in the room. And Jesus commended her faith.

Likewise, the widow who came to the temple to worship, putting only a small amount in the offering, caught the eye of the Savior.

"Jesus sat down opposite the place where the offerings were put and watched the crowd putting their money into the temple treasury. Many rich people threw in large amounts. but a poor widow came and put in two very small copper coins, worth only a fraction of a penny" (Mark 12:41-42).

Can you imagine how she could have felt, following behind those who just "threw" in their large amounts of money? But the widow came with the right heart. She didn't care what they thought of her worship.

> "Calling his disciples to him, Jesus said, 'I tell you the truth, this poor widow has put more into the treasury than all the others. They all gave out of their wealth; but she, out of her poverty, put in everything—all she had to live on'" (Mark 12:43-44).

That's how we should bring our worship to God—giving everything we've got, not worried about what others think, with our hearts focused, not on ourselves, but on our God. When we do, our worship will be commended by God, but we will also set an example for others that points to Him.

> "'In the same way, let your light shine before men, that they may see your good deeds and praise your Father in heaven'" (Matthew 5:16).

This verse isn't about doing acts of righteousness in order to be seen; Jesus goes on right after that to say that we should be careful NOT to do them to be seen (6:1). Letting our light shine means that we live a life of worship that points to Him, not to us.

Women who truly worship may erupt in praise like Hannah or Mary, but it won't be about them. Their hearts will be focused on God. They may be bold in their worship like Miriam, but they won't care what others think because it's not about them. And their worship may sometimes seem extravagant like the sinful woman or not enough like the poor widow, but like Miriam, they will lead on anyway. Because their God is worth it.

What about you and me? Will we be willing to give God the praise He is due, even if it makes us uncomfortable? Or if it makes others uncomfortable? Are we willing to be extravagant in our worship, giving all that we have? And are we setting an example of worship in spirit and in truth that will be a witness to those around us of our great God?

My prayer for you and me is that we will be women who worship, regardless of our own weaknesses, regardless of what others think, and regardless of how little or much we think we have to bring. It's the very thing we were created for.

> "Therefore, since we are receiving a kingdom that cannot be shaken, let us be thankful, and so worship God acceptably with reverence and awe, for our 'God is a consuming fire'" (Hebrews 12:28-29).

Let's be women who worship—unhindered, unashamed, and undeniably in love with Jesus.

DO I HAVE
ANYTHING TO GIVE?:
TABITHA

She isn't that well-known as far as women of the Bible go. She doesn't have the notoriety of Ruth, Esther, Sarah, or Mary; but she is important. And she has an important lesson for us today.

> "In Joppa there was a disciple named Tabitha (which, when translated, is Dorcas), who was always doing good and helping the poor. About that time she became sick and died, and her body was washed and placed in an upstairs room. Lydda was near Joppa; so when the disciples heard that Peter was in Lydda, they sent two men to him and urged him, 'Please come at once!'" (Acts 9:36-38).

Tabitha was her Aramaic name, which is probably what she was known by. Dorcas was the translation in Greek, which is what Luke was writing in because Greek became a common language among the people of that time.

Tabitha was a disciple of Christ known for "doing good and helping the poor." We already know that many women followed Jesus as His disciples. They sat at His feet, learned from Him, and supported Him out of their own means (Luke 8:1-3).

But here we see a woman who was known not just as a believer but as one who truly served others. Her love for Christ and for her brothers and sisters compelled her to put that love into action and do something.

Tabitha could have reasoned that since she wasn't a leader like Priscilla (Acts 18), a church planter like Lydia (Acts 16:11-15, 40), or a prophetess like one of Phillip's daughters (Acts 21:8-9), then she had nothing to give. Instead, she used the abilities she did have to serve God—so much so that her death was a huge blow to the new community of faith.

> "Peter went with them, and when he arrived he was taken upstairs to the room. All the widows stood around him, crying and showing him the robes and other clothing that Dorcas had made while she was still with them" (Acts 9:39).

Maybe Dorcas couldn't lead worship, write a book, or grace a stage with a speaking gift, but she could sew. And she used that gift to serve God and the people around her. They mourned her loss because her presence and her heart and her gifts were important to their community. She blessed people. Her love made others' lives better. And that mattered.

> "Peter sent them all out of the room; then he got down on his knees and prayed. Turning toward the dead woman, he said, 'Tabitha, get up.' she opened her eyes, and seeing Peter she sat up. He took her by the hand and helped her to her feet. Then he called the believers and the widows and presented her to them alive" (Acts 9:40-41).

You know, not every person who died during the early church ministry was raised back to life. But Tabitha was. Her ministry was so significant that the disciples felt the need to call on Peter. And Peter felt the need to call on God.

I don't know what your gifts, talents, or abilities are, but I know this: God will honor what you have when you offer it in His name. You don't have to feel confident or be successful. He just calls us to be faithful (1 Corinthians 15:58).

And He alone determines the gifts and abilities He gives (Romans 12:18). Our job is to use them in service to Him and others, trusting Him with the results.

"This became known all over Joppa, and many people believed in the Lord" (Acts 9:42).

Wow! God used Tabitha's life to draw many people to Him. That's the ultimate use of any abilities God has given us. All because she was willing to use what she had—needle, thread, and a willing heart.

What gift or ability has God given you? Maybe you can cook, pray, or give great hugs. As my friend Michelle says, "Nothing is wasted in God's Kingdom." Big or small, God can do great things with a heart devoted to Him. Surrender what you have, and let Him use it for His glory.

UNITY OF PURPOSE:
EUODIA AND SYNTYCHE

Have you ever had a disagreement with someone at church, and it changed not only your relationship, but the whole dynamic of church? Suddenly, you're no longer happy there, the atmosphere changes, and your desire to worship wanes.

I once was so offended by something said to me at church that I stopped going for about a month. I visited other churches, but my heart was so wounded, I didn't want to go back to my own church.

It wasn't even a personal affront. It was a statement about someone else that I found so offensive, I fell into the enemy's trap of judgment, criticism, and disdain toward not only the person who said it, but toward all those in the church I assumed agreed with the same philosophy.

Perhaps you've been in a similar situation and allowed the affront to cause you to withdraw, criticize, or gossip.

Maybe it wasn't even something all that important, but suddenly you feel hurt or no longer included among a group of friends. Or maybe you are the one who has some issue with another person, and it keeps you from worshiping God as you know you should.

One thing I love about the Word of God is that we can always find answers for the problems we face in its pages. Paul once addressed a similar situation in the church at Philippi.

> "I plead with Euodia and I plead with Syntyche to agree with each other in the Lord. Yes, and I ask you, loyal yokefellow, help these women who have contended at my side in the cause of the gospel, along with Clement and the rest of my fellow workers, whose names are in the book of life" (Philippians 4:2-3).

Let's look at three things we can learn from this snippet of Paul's letter to the church at Philippi.

First, disagreements need to be addressed.

The disagreement between these two women was serious enough that Paul felt the need to address it from prison in a letter that was to be read to the whole church. I think if we stopped sometimes to truly think about why we're upset, offended, or disagreeable, we would realize that it's not worth bringing division within the body.

If our disagreements were brought before the whole church we might think twice about holding onto them! The truth is that even petty disagreements can cause major strife and division within the church. And Satan loves to divide and distract us from our mission of loving God and loving others.

Paul knew that if these two women did not agree with one another, the church would suffer as a whole. If one woman decided to leave the fellowship, more disunity could follow, and the growth of the church would be hindered.

Second, disagreements can be overcome.

Paul knew these women well enough to believe that with a little encouragement, they would set aside their differences and come to an agreement. These were women who had served beside him in ministry. He knew their hearts and their desire to serve the Lord. Paul was confident they could be persuaded to lay aside their differences for the sake of the kingdom.

"...then make my joy complete by being like-minded, having the same love, being one in spirit and purpose" (Philippians 2:2).

Throughout his letters, Paul encourages the pursuit of unity, peace, and humility towards others.

Third, some matters are disputable.

Paul doesn't take sides, which means their disagreement wasn't a matter of doctrinal truth. If it had been, Paul would have clearly pointed out who was right and who was wrong in the situation.

There will be times that we disagree with someone over a doctrinal issue that must be addressed. We should always stand firm on the truth of God's Word and be willing to confront any error. But most of the time, our disagreements are over areas of offense that can be worked out.

In my situation, I took one comment and judged someone's heart and intention based on it, rather than taking the time to talk to the person about what they meant and how we should view it from a biblical perspective.

JUST LIKE US

We sometimes tend to judge the heart and intentions of others based on something they said or did. But we can't know what is in another's heart. We shouldn't assume the worst but instead think the best of our brothers and sisters in the Lord and have genuine conversations with them.

"Make every effort to keep the unity of the Spirit through the bond of peace. There is one body and one Spirit—just as you were called to one hope when you were called—one Lord, one faith, one baptism; one God and Father of all, who is over all and through all and in all" (Ephesians 4:3-6).

Oftentimes, we fail to understand that we are all at different stages of growth in our walk with the Lord. We need to give others grace to grow and be patient with them as they learn.

"Accept him whose faith is weak, without passing judgment on disputable matters" (Romans 14:1).

Disputable matters are those things that don't change the gospel message. Even if we think we are right, we can choose to lay down our opinion for the sake of the gospel. Rather than striving to be right, judging one another, or spreading gossip, we can actually agree with one another and move on.

Agreeing with one another doesn't mean one party has to give up her position, but rather we agree together in our purpose, and that is to serve Christ together as one.

Jesus Himself prayed that we would be one as He and the Father are one (John 17:20-23). We may not always agree on an issue, but we can agree to serve God together, contending side by side for the gospel.

Growing in spiritual maturity means that we give up our right to be right and love others with humility and grace. Is there someone with whom you need to agree together in the Lord for the sake of the church and the gospel? Is holding onto that offense worth the unity of your church?

> "May the God who gives endurance and encouragement give you a spirit of unity among yourselves as you follow Christ Jesus, so that with one heart and mouth you may glorify the God and Father of our Lord Jesus Christ" (Romans 15:5-6).

Let's be women who walk in spiritual maturity, willing to lay aside our differences, give others grace to grow, and assume the best in each other. Then we can focus on the mission God has called us to in Christ Jesus. Lives may very well depend on it.

THE SEARCH FOR FAITH

IN A WORLD OF DOUBT

SEEKING TO PLEASE GOD: MRS. NOAH

———————— ⟨∽⟩ ————————

Have you ever wondered what it was like for Noah's wife? To spend over a year on an ark with all those animals, feeding them, and smelling them every day? We think our house is a zoo. We have no idea.

But then after a year cooped up on the ark, can you imagine stepping out onto a fresh, new world, clean, pure, and quiet? Man, the potential. Yet, the renewed earth they looked out on still wasn't Eden—and they still had the potential to sin.

Like the people of Noah's day, our sin also deserves judgment. Just as Noah's family found refuge in the ark, we find refuge in Jesus. When we come to Christ in faith and repentance, He cleanses us from all our sin and shame. He washes us as clean and pure as that fresh earth after the rushing waters purged the evil and darkness from the land.

> "Therefore, if anyone is in Christ, he is a new creation; the old has gone, the new has come!" (2 Corinthians 5:17).

Yet, we still have the potential to sin. We are redeemed but not yet made perfect. We are citizens of a new kingdom and yet still abide here on earth. I imagine Mrs. Noah was disappointed to find that even after the cleansing flood, sin was still right there with them. The world was new and yet still the same.

In Christ, we are new creations, but our challenge is to not conform to the world from which we were rescued.

"Therefore, I urge you, brothers, in view of God's mercy, to offer your bodies as living sacrifices, holy and pleasing to God—this is your spiritual act of worship. Do not conform any longer to the pattern of this world, but be transformed by the renewing of your mind" (Romans 12:1-2).

Jesus is our sacrifice for sin, but that fact doesn't absolve us of the responsibility to choose obedience. We are called to be living sacrifices and to not conform to the ways of the world. I don't know about you, but that is a daily struggle for me. I desire to do what is right, yet my heart can be so easily led astray by my own selfishness, pride, and greed.

And the world can sometimes seem so appealing.

"Do not love the world or anything in the world. If anyone loves the world, the love of the Father is not in him. For everything in the world—the cravings of sinful man, the lust of his eyes and the boasting of what he has and does—comes not from the Father but from the world. The world and its desires pass away, but the man who does the will of God lives forever" (1 John 2:15-17).

John is not talking about loving the people of the world, such as in John 3:16 when he said, "God so loved the world...." Instead, he is referring to the world of sin controlled by the devil. Think about it:

our sinful cravings, the worldly things that look good to us, and the boasting of who we think we are or what we think we have—none of that brings glory to God. It's sin, plain and simple.

So, how can we live each day as new creations bringing glory to God?

First, we have to have a heart that *wants* to please God. If we belong to Jesus, our desire to please Him should outweigh all other desires.

> "Jesus replied: 'Love the Lord your God with all your heart and with all your soul and with all your mind'" (Matthew 22:37).

Second, we need to renew our minds in the Word. The more time we spend in the Word, the more our hearts and minds become aligned with God's values.

> "Those who live according to the sinful nature have their minds set on what that nature desires; but those who live in accordance with the Spirit have their minds set on what the Spirit desires" (Romans 8:5).

Third, empowered by His Spirit, we choose. That's right. We have to choose to do the right thing, even when it hurts our flesh and makes us uncomfortable.

> "Do not merely listen to the word and so deceive yourselves. Do what it says" (James 1:22).

We may have to turn off the TV or computer, separate ourselves from ungodly relationships, or walk away from gossip. We may have to choose to set aside that little extra sleep to spend time with God; we may have to choose to close our mouths when we want to complain or argue; we may have to choose to let our spouse be right.

We may have to choose to not tell the lie that makes us look better; we may have to choose to turn the other cheek; we may have to choose to humble ourselves and let others be first. Obedience is not our default setting. We have to be intentional to choose to obey. We do so because we love God, and we want to please Him.

And when we mess up, we 'fess up. We admit our sinfulness, accept His forgiveness, and continue on our journey with Him, growing from faith to faith.

> "Submit yourselves, then, to God. Resist the devil, and he will flee from you. Come near to God and he will come to near to you" (James 4:7-8a).

Obedience doesn't come natural to our flesh, but it is the desire of our spirit if we belong to Jesus. And every day His mercies are new (Lamentations 3:22-23). Like Noah's wife, we run to the refuge of Jesus for salvation, and we step out into a new creation by faith— one that is groaning as it awaits the day when we will be made perfect forever (Romans 8:20-23).

What sin are you struggling to overcome? Confess it, resist it, and run into the arms of Your Father. Then continue on your journey as you follow hard after Him in faith.

SURVIVING DOUBT
AND CONFUSION:
SARAH

———————— ∞ ————————

Many years ago I had a friend who was diagnosed with cancer. We prayed and believed with all the faith that was within us that she would be healed, but she wasn't—at least not the way we had hoped. For several years after that, I struggled with doubt and confusion. If God tells us to believe, to trust, to walk by faith, why does life not always work out the way we believed?

One thing I love about the Word of God is that we find people there who struggled with the same issues we do. And they didn't always handle them the right way, which is even more evidence to me that this Bible I'm holding is real. If it were made up, someone should have gone to a little more trouble for everything to always be perfect and for the followers of God to always do the right thing, don't you think?

But no, they are so very real, just like us.

When I look at the story of Sarah, I always tend to judge her too quickly, as if I would never make the same choices she did. But, umm, I do. A lot. Leaving behind everything she knew and all the comforts of home, Sarah set out with Abraham to a place they had never been or seen before. She followed her man, even when it took her to unfamiliar territory.

But God met them right there and promised them a future.

"The LORD appeared to Abram and said, 'To your offspring I will give this land.' So he built an altar there to the LORD, who had appeared to him" (Genesis 12:7).

Then, guess what? No food. Yep, they left everything behind at the ripe old ages of 75 for Abraham and 65 for Sarah (who were still called Abram and Sarai at that point), and ended up in a land of famine.

So, Abraham led his crew down to Egypt where the Nile kept things pretty fertile. Only, Sarah was rocking it at 65—so beautiful that Abraham told her to claim she was his sister so he wouldn't be killed.

Pharaoh found out about her beauty and had her brought to join his harem. Because they thought Abraham was her brother, his life was spared.

But Sarah was trapped at the palace, about to become another concubine to the Egyptian king. Then God intervened.

"But the LORD inflicted serious diseases on Pharaoh and his household because of Abram's wife Sarai. So Pharaoh summoned Abram.

'What have you done to me?' he said. 'Why didn't you tell me she was your wife? Why did you say, "She is my sister," so that I took her to be my wife? Now then, here is your wife. Take her and go!'" (Genesis 12:17-19).

I imagine spending some time in an Egyptian harem was a little shaky for Sarah, but God took care of her and protected her from Pharaoh's advances. Ten years later, Sarah was still waiting for that promise of God to be fulfilled. At seventy-five, she was still barren. That promise of offspring probably seemed like a distant dream.

Sarah began to believe that God wanted her to carry out the promise with her own plan.

"...so she said to Abram, 'The LORD has kept me from having children. Go, sleep with my maidservant; perhaps I can build a family through her'" (Genesis 16:2a).

Well, I guess I can't blame her. How many times have I "hunted down a Hagar" as my friend Michelle says? Often, when God doesn't seem to be answering according to my plans and my timeline, I figure He needs me to intervene with a "better" plan.

It worked for Sarah—at least temporarily. Her maidservant Hagar did bear Abraham a son. But not only was he not the son of the promise, his conception only caused Sarah more trouble, as Hagar began to despise her. Feeling unappreciated, Sarah complained to Abraham, who told her to deal with her own mess (16:6). Sarah only made matters worse by mistreating her maidservant.

Sarah followed her husband in faith to an unfamiliar land, ended up in an unfair situation at the palace of Pharaoh, tried to fix an unfulfilled promise with her own plan, and was left unappreciated by her maidservant and her husband when her plan didn't quite work out the way she thought.

I imagine she was wracked with doubt and confusion.

"Why God? Why would you lead us to a place where there was no food, send us to Egypt for me to be kidnapped, deliver me from Pharaoh but not deliver the promise, and let me mess it all up with my own plan?"

Have you ever felt that way? Have you ever tried to follow God, but the way He led seemed to be worse than where you were before? Have you ever felt you had a promise from God, but years later, you are still waiting? Have you ever tried to take matters into your own hands to "help" God bring your promises to pass, only to make things much worse?

We all have been Sarah at some point and time. The beautiful thing about her story is that God never abandoned her, continued to work in every situation, and never failed to keep His promise.

> "God also said to Abraham, 'As for Sarai your wife, you are no longer to call her Sarai; her name will be Sarah. I will bless her and will surely give you a son by her. I will bless her so that she will be the mother of nations; kings of peoples will come from her'" (Genesis 17:15-16).

God is faithful.

He renewed his covenant with Abraham, this time including Sarah specifically in the promise. Fifteen more years had gone by, but

God was faithful. He fulfilled His promise to Abraham and still used Sarah to do it.

> "Now the LORD was gracious to Sarah as he had said, and the LORD did for Sarah what he had promised. Sarah became pregnant and bore a son to Abraham in his old age, at the very time God had promised him" (Genesis 21:1-2).

God is gracious.

We may not always understand God's promise, His plan, or His timing, but we can be sure that He is faithful and He is gracious. Every Word He has spoken will come to pass. His promises cannot be broken. It's just who He is. And when we fail to understand, He is gracious still.

I don't know why my friend's healing came in the form of eternity. I don't always understand how faith works. But I do know that God is good and God is love. Sarah may not have always believed perfectly, but God calls her faithful.

> "By faith, Sarah herself received power to conceive, even when she was past the age, since she considered him faithful who had promised" (Hebrews 11:11, ESV).

Even when we struggle with doubt and confusion, God will be faithful to meet us right where we are with grace. And He will fulfill every promise in His Word. Our best. His way. Our good. His glory.

PASSING ON THE FAITH: LOIS AND EUNICE

———————— ⌒ ————————

When I first decided to follow Jesus, I was still in college. Three years later I was married. During those three years, I craved the presence of God. I read the Bible, hungry for truth. And the more I read, the more of His life I wanted in mine.

So, I was determined that I would raise my future children in a Christian home, where God was the center of our lives. When I read the Great Commission (Matthew 28:19-20) to go and make disciples, I wanted my children to be those first disciples that I could pour my heart into.

In one of Paul's letters to Timothy, we get a glimpse of two women who did the same. They brought Timothy up with sincere faith in their hearts for God which was later reflected in his own life.

> "I have been reminded of your sincere faith, which first lived in your grandmother Lois and in your mother Eunice and, I am persuaded, now lives in you also" (2 Timothy 1:5).

I love that we get this little glimpse into the lives of the parents who helped shape the faith of Timothy, a young man who became like a son to Paul and to whom Paul had entrusted the church at

Ephesus. Timothy's mother was a Jewish Christian and his father was Greek.

> "He [Paul] came to Derbe and then to Lystra, where a disciple named Timothy lived, whose mother was a Jewess and a believer, but whose father was a Greek" (Acts 16:1).

Commentators believe that because Scripture emphasizes his mother's belief and not his father's, that Timothy's father was not a believer. It is also believed that, because Paul references Timothy fifteen years later as a young man (1 Timothy 4:12), that he was actually a teen at this time. So, we get this little glimpse into the life of a young man whose mother and grandmother influenced him to believe in God, even at a young age and also having had an unbelieving father.

I want to share with you three approaches we can take as moms to help disciple our children in the ways of the Lord.

First, we teach them the Word.

I think we sometimes believe that our kids should get their Bible teaching from church and Sunday school, but the first place they should learn the Word is at home. In Paul's letter to Timothy, he reminds him to continue in the Word he had been taught from infancy.

> "But as for you, continue in what you have learned and have become convinced of, because you know those from whom you learned it, and how from infancy you have known the holy Scriptures, which are able to make you wise for salvation through faith in Christ Jesus" (2 Timothy 3:14-15).

121

As parents, we should be the primary teachers of the Word to our children. We can do so through bedtime devotions, family worship, or dinner table talks. As we go through daily life—in the car, at the market, etc.—we have the opportunity to use the Scripture to enforce life lessons.

> "These commandments that I give you today are to be upon your hearts. Impress them on your children. Talk about them when you sit at home and when you walk along the road, when you lie down and when you get up" (Deuteronomy 6:6-7).

Second, pray with your children.

We all pray *for* our children, but I believe it is so important that they hear us pray aloud *with* them. When we do, they hear our heart for them to know Christ and walk with Him. We are reinforcing our love for them and establishing their identity in Jesus.

In Hebrew culture, the blessing of children was a big deal (Think Esau and Jacob). In their book, *Giving the Blessing: Daily Thoughts on the Joy of Giving,* Gary Smalley and John Trent describe what the blessing meant to Jewish families in Old Testament times.

"For sons or daughters in biblical times, receiving the blessing was a momentous event. At a specific point in their lives they would hear their parents pronounce words of encouragement, love, and acceptance. They would hear their names linked with God's promises and the special history of their people."[9]

I believe this blessing should be part of our prayers over our children, so they grow and develop with an understanding that they are loved and cherished by their Creator.

> "People were bringing little children to Jesus to have him touch them, but the disciples rebuked them. When Jesus saw this, he was indignant. He said to them, 'Let the little children come to me, and do not hinder them, for the kingdom of God belongs to such as these. I tell you the truth, anyone who will not receive the kingdom of God like a little child will never enter it.' And he took the children in his arms, put his hands on them and blessed them" (Mark 10:14).

Third, lead by example.

I realize this point is the most difficult to carry out, but with God's help we can do our best. Many young people raised in church fall away when they become old enough to decide for themselves. Often, the reason is that they witnessed a different message between church and home.

As Christian parents, we are not perfect; but I don't believe that is an excuse to be lazy in our spiritual growth. We need to live what we believe and own it when we mess up. My children still tell me I angrily threw a chair one day when we were home schooling. I have no recollection of that, but the fact they laugh about it gives me hope that I at least made it right with them later!

Being an example is not about being the perfect mom all the time; it's about spending quiet time with the Lord every day, walking in the Spirit with God's grace, and being quick to ask forgiveness when we do mess up.

"For I am not seeking my own good but the good of many, so that they may be saved. Follow my example, as I follow the example of Christ" (1 Corinthians 10:33b-11:1).

Making disciples is about setting an example for others to follow. So as moms, we can learn from the example of Lois and Eunice, who "from infancy" taught Timothy the ways of the Lord. I'm sure they weren't perfect, but Scripture says they were sincere.

Maybe you didn't have a great example yourself. Maybe your child-rearing days are behind you, and you have many regrets. I would encourage you to talk with your children, confessing your sins, and asking for their forgiveness.

You are not responsible for their response but only your obedience. So, be encouraged, because the God we serve is more than able to redeem your past mistakes. In fact, that's what He does best.

PRAYING WITH EXPECTATION AFTER DISAPPOINTMENT: RHODA

⎯⎯⎯⎯⎯ ⟲⟳ ⎯⎯⎯⎯⎯

Have you ever been praying for something, but then you realize you keep talking about the situation as if nothing is going to change? Sometimes it's really hard to believe things will change. Disappointments in the past can color the way we view our present circumstance.

I get tickled every time I read this story in Acts about Peter's miraculous escape from prison. Oh, there was nothing funny about Peter's arrest—especially since Herod had just had the apostle James put to death (Acts 12:2). I'm sure at the time of Peter's arrest, the early church feared for his very life.

> "So Peter was kept in prison, but the church was praying earnestly to God for him" (Acts 12:5).

I wonder what it was like for the believers that night as they prayed. This event occurred about ten years after Jesus' death and resurrection. James had been beheaded just like John the Baptist. Stephen had been stoned.

The early church had witnessed persecution; but they had also witnessed miracles. In fact, they had seen the angel of the Lord deliver the apostles from jail before (Acts 5:17-42). So here they were again, earnestly praying that God would intervene and save Peter's life, yet knowing that God may choose not to should that be His will, as in the case of James and Stephen.

How do we hold that tension between faith that God will answer our prayer and the knowledge that it may not be His will? And why bother praying if God is going to do what He wants anyway? Have you ever struggled with these thoughts?

I have prayed earnestly for a friend's healing with faith and expectation, only to watch her die. But I have also prayed with fervor for a friend whom God chose to heal. I'll be honest. It messes with your head.

When we know God has the power to do something, but it's not always His will, how do we continue to believe the next time in a way that exhibits faith?

In our story with Peter, God does answer their pleas. Once again, an angel of the Lord showed up and led Peter out of the prison. He found his way to the house of John Mark's mother, where many had gathered to pray.

> "Peter knocked at the outer entrance, and a servant girl named Rhoda came to answer the door. When she recognized Peter's voice, she was so overjoyed she ran back without opening it and exclaimed, 'Peter is at the door!'" (Acts 12:13-14).

This is where I get tickled. Here they have been praying all night for Peter's release, but when he shows up, they slam the door in his face. The Greek used here for servant girl signifies a young girl or damsel, not quite of marriageable age, so late childhood. She knew Peter's voice, so she was familiar with the apostle and probably was part of the early church.

Rhoda knew they were witnessing a miracle and got so excited, she forgot to let Peter in! Have you ever been surprised by God? Have you witnessed His answer before in a way that caused you to almost not believe it?

> "'You're out of your mind,' they told her. When she kept insisting that it was so, they said, 'It must be his angel'" (Acts 12:15).

By this time, the church had witnessed great persecution. I'm sure they had prayed fervently for James the apostle, son of Zebedee. Yet their brother James, who had walked with Jesus as one of the Twelve, had been executed.

It's so easy to become disappointed when our prayers don't get answered the way we want. And sometimes we are afraid to believe again because we don't want to experience the same heartache. But God wants us to continue to believe Him to do the impossible. He doesn't want us to give up on prayer. He wants us to trust Him.

With God, all things are possible, but not all things are within His plan for us. Rather than putting our faith in what God can do, we have to put our faith in the God who can.

So, instead of focusing on our situation, we focus on our God. Instead of talking about the problem, we talk about Jesus. Rather than praying with doubt, we pray with faith that our God loves us and does what is best for us, and in Him we can trust.

We will all struggle with disappointments and prayers that don't seem to go our way. Even Jesus prayed in the garden:

"'Father, if you are willing, take this cup from me...'" (Luke 22:42a).

Yet He trusted the Father's love for Him:

"'...yet not my will, but yours be done'" (Luke 22:42b).

So, how do we hold this tension between knowing God can and wondering if He will? We look to the Word of God which teaches us both the sovereignty of God and the responsibility of man. Throughout the Bible we find Scriptures that attest to the sovereign will of God (Colossians 1), yet we also find many calls to persevere in prayer (Luke 11:1-13).

Bible scholar D.A. Carson puts it like this:

"The perverse and the unbeliever will appeal to God's sovereignty to urge the futility of prayer in a determined universe; they will appeal to passages depicting God as a person (including those that speak of his relenting) to infer that he is weak, fickle, and impotent, once again concluding that it is useless to pray. But the faithful will insist that properly handled, both God's sovereignty and his personhood become reasons for more prayer, not reasons for abandoning prayer. It is worth praying to a sovereign God because he is free and can take action as he wills; it is worth praying to a personal God because he hears, responds, and acts on behalf of his people, not according to the blind rigidities of inexorable fate." [10]

God loves us and works His will in our lives, of that we can be sure. Therefore, in our darkest hour, we can trust Him and pray earnestly with faith, believing that if it is in His power and for our good, we have what we have asked for (1 John 5:14-15).

So, don't stop praying and trusting God with your situation. A miracle might be right outside the door.

DON'T GIVE UP:
THE PERSISTENT WIDOW

When you have prayed, fasted, worshiped, obeyed, and called on the Lord in every way you know how, and the answer still doesn't come, what do you do?

If you are like me, you cry and complain and look for someone to listen to your struggles and hopefully share a word that will make you feel better. And when that doesn't help, you begin to doubt yourself and wonder what you've done wrong or how you missed Him.

It's hard not to just give up in despair. Today as I was deep in prayer on this subject, I thought about the Parable of the Persistent Widow.

> "Then Jesus told his disciples a parable to show them that they should always pray and not give up" (Luke 18:1).

I love that we get the reason for the parable in the first sentence—that we should "always pray and not give up."

Keep coming to Jesus.

> "He said, 'In a certain town there was a judge who neither feared God nor cared about men. And there was a widow in

that town who kept coming to him with the plea, "Grant me justice against my adversary"'" (Luke 18:2-3).

Jesus shared this story with His disciples and used a widow as His main character. A widow in those days represented the poorest and most vulnerable of society, because without a husband, she had no one to care for her needs or seek justice on her behalf.

Not only that, but she was dealing with both an adversary and an unworthy judge who didn't fear God nor care about others. We aren't told anything regarding her foe or how she had been wronged, but only that she sought justice against her adversary.

We too have an adversary.

"Be self-controlled and alert. Your enemy the devil prowls around like a roaring lion, looking for someone to devour" (1 Peter 5:8).

Be watchful.

Sometimes we blame the devil for every problem we face, when many of our troubles are the result of our own choices. But sometimes we do the opposite: We blame ourselves for every problem and fail to see the enemy behind the scenes wreaking havoc.

We must be watchful for the work of the enemy in our lives, seeking the Father to come to our aid and work on our behalf. Thank God, we have a better Judge than the one in this story.

"'For some time he refused. But finally he said to himself, "Even though I don't fear God or care about men, yet because this widow keeps bothering me, I will see that she gets justice, so that she won't eventually wear me out with her coming!'"' (Luke 18:4-5).

I love it! She refused to give up or give in. She would not lose heart. She continued to cry out for justice against her adversary because she believed.

Don't give up!

Sometimes, we get so weary and tired of the battle that we are tempted to throw our hands up and just say, "You win, Devil." But Jesus told this parable so we would not lose heart!

> "'And the Lord said, 'Listen to what the unrighteous judge says. And will not God bring about justice for his chosen ones, who cry out to him day and night? Will he keep putting them off? I tell you, he will see that they get justice, and quickly'" (Luke 18:6-8a).

If a judge who doesn't love God or people will give in to faith and persistence, how much more will a loving God give His children justice against our enemy? You may feel that you have been crying out day and night already. You might read this and think, "Well, God has obviously forgotten about me because I'm still waiting for an answer."

Listen. God is the Righteous Judge. And what may seem slow in coming to us is right on time with Him. What looks like a "no" to our requests is always God working for our good, even when we can't see it and don't feel it (Romans 8:28).

What seem to be failure and darkness and despair all around us are just the clouds obscuring the brightness of the sun. He is still here. He is with us. And He is working on our behalf (Romans 8:34).

> "'However, when the Son of Man comes, will he find faith on the earth?'" (Luke 18:8).

That's the real question.

Jesus told this parable in the context of a discussion with His disciples about His second coming. It was a warning to them that in the last days many would be going on with life as if they had nothing to fear, living for themselves without a care in the world. He reminded them as He had taught them before that "whoever tries to keep his life will lose it, and whoever loses his life will preserve it" (17:33).

Have faith in God.

Jesus was teaching us to keep our focus on Him, even unto death, even when things look bad, even when the answers don't come. We live for Him and we pray and we don't give up. Even in the face of suffering and unanswered questions, we don't lose heart. Because the adversary is real, and he's relentless. But he's not victorious.

We are victorious (1 John 5:4). We are redeemed (Galatians 3:13). We are the overcomers (1 John 4:4). We are seated in heavenly places (Ephesians 2:6), co-heirs with Christ (Romans 8:17), and promised an eternity that far outweighs the troubles and trials of this world (2 Corinthians 4:17).

We just have to believe it.

> "Resist him [the devil], standing firm in your faith, because you know that your brothers throughout the world are undergoing the same kind of sufferings. And the God of all grace who called you to his eternal glory in Christ, after you have suffered a little while, will himself restore you and make you strong, firm, and steadfast. To him be the power forever and ever. Amen" (1 Peter 5:9-11).

Yes ma'am. You just keep crying out to Jesus. He will find faith on this earth.

SEEKING THE BEST FOR OUR KIDS: SALOME

When our son left for college, he was planning to become a profiler with the FBI—maybe not the highest-paying job out there, but certainly one that comes with a measure of status.

After about a month at Liberty University, he told us the Lord had called him to full-time missions. This mama's heart was so happy that he was following the call of God on his life, yet also anxious about what that might look like in a world that is increasingly intolerant of Christianity.

I'll admit, we had friends who questioned his choice—the work will be dangerous, difficult, and with very little monetary reward.

Part of being good mamas is wanting the best for our kiddos. We want the best schools, teams, and clubs for them. We pray for them, teach them, and do our best to set an example for them of what it means to follow Christ.

But what happens when God calls them to something that isn't necessarily safe or doesn't look like success in the world's eyes? Will we ask the Lord to grant them favor, or will we trust them in His hands?

Salome was a woman who loved and followed Jesus (Mark 15:40-41). She was one of the women who stayed with Him at the cross (Matthew 27:55-5). She is also a woman who allowed her love for her sons to cloud her understanding of Jesus' kingdom and what it meant for her boys to serve Him.

> "Then the mother of Zebedee's sons came to Jesus with her sons and, kneeling down, asked a favor of him.
>
> 'What is it you want?' he asked.
>
> She said, 'Grant that one of these two sons of mine may sit at your right and the other at your left in your kingdom'" (Matthew 20:20-21).

We have to understand that like most of the Jews in her day, Salome probably believed that the Messiah would set up His kingdom on earth and deliver God's people from the hands of the Roman Empire.

Her request wasn't as outlandish as it may at first seem. She probably had already noticed that her sons, James and John, were part of Jesus' inner circle (Matthew 17:1-2, Matthew 26:36-39, Luke 8:50-55), and therefore her request would have been a reasonable one.

Oh, I know her heart! Don't we so want the best for our children? We want them to be successful and ambitious, perhaps obtaining higher salaries or having greater opportunities than we did. Salome, however, didn't consider the ramifications of what following Jesus really meant.

"'You don't know what you are asking,' Jesus said to them. 'Can you drink the cup I am going to drink?'"

'We can,' they answered.

Jesus said to them, 'You will indeed drink from my cup, but to sit at my right or left is not for me to grant. These places belong to those for whom they have been prepared by my Father'" (Matthew 20:22-23).

We know that Jesus was referring to the cup of suffering. And from history, we also know that James was the first disciple to be martyred. John was eventually exiled to the island of Patmos. Following Jesus wasn't the easiest or safest path to take in life.

If we want God's best for our children, we have to consider that His plan for them may not be as safe and comfy and prosperous as what we really want for them. And if they go into full-time ministry, we may still desire for them to obtain a good position, be in a safe location, and not be far away from us. I have to admit, I have often prayed for that.

But you know, I think God understands. Jesus didn't rebuke Salome. He just asked the boys if they realized what they were getting into. He told them they would indeed face suffering if they continued on with Him. Jesus used their desire to reign with Him as a lesson in what it really means to serve.

"Jesus called them together and said, 'You know that the rulers of the Gentiles lord it over them, and their high officials exercise authority over them. Not so with you. Instead, whoever wants to become great among you must be your

servant, and whoever wants to be first must be your slave—
just as the Son of Man did not come to be served, but to give
his life as a ransom for many"' (Matthew 20:25-28).

We want our kids to become great, to be first in school, on the ball
field, and in social clubs. We want the very best in life for our
children, just as Salome wanted for her boys. But if we truly want
them to follow Jesus, we have to remember that in God's
Kingdom, that looks like service, not necessarily high salaries.
Following Jesus means sacrifice, not necessarily status and success.

Just as Salome had to trust God with James and John, we have to
trust Him with our children, understanding that this life isn't all
there is. If we want to raise kids who love God and make a
difference in the world, then we have to let go of our idea of what
that looks like and trust His plan for them.

The disciples of Jesus were all persecuted, but their influence is still
felt today. We have much of the New Testament because of the
eyewitness accounts of these men and the writings of some of
them, including Salome's boy John, who wrote the Gospel of John,
1, 2, and 3 John, and the Revelation.

When we encourage our children to follow Jesus, we must accept
His plans for them, even if that means letting go of our own ideas
about their futures. But when we give them the freedom and
support to follow the call wherever it leads, they flourish in His
plans.

Remember, Salome was among those women who stayed with
Jesus at the cross and was there at the empty tomb. She may have
had to deal with some harsh realities about the cost of following

Jesus, but she had also experienced the reality of His death and resurrection.

When we fully grasp the majesty and power of God, we will understand that He is sovereign over all things. Our children are a blessing from God, and we have the opportunity to raise them in His ways (Deuteronomy 6:4-9, Proverbs 22:6).

But if we truly believe that God is who He says He is, we can also trust Him with their lives and their futures. Because when we truly understand who Jesus is, there's no better way than His way. I think even Salome would agree.

SIDE BY SIDE
FOR THE GOSPEL:
PRISCILLA

———————— ∽ ————————

I'll never forget our time in Guatemala in 2005. Kenneth and I were given the opportunity to go and share God's love alongside missionaries who were serving there full-time. Kenneth had never flown and was very nervous about it, but he agreed to go anyway. We stayed in a beautiful place in Antigua, then traveled with our group to villages each day to minister through medical care, clothing, food, and the gospel, which was shared at the end of each day.

I could tell many God stories of events that took place, lives that were changed, hungry mouths that were fed. I could also share some funny moments that would make you laugh.

But what I want to share today is the power of serving God side by side with my spouse. I can honestly say that those are the moments that mean more in our marriage than anything else. I recall our serving as "pharmacists"—Kenneth's counting out pills and my mixing cough syrup as we assisted the medical staff.

I can still see the children, the mamas and daddies, the hearts and tummies that were fed, the eyes that were opened, wounds healed.

I can smell the scent of freshly-made tortillas, feel the sweat pouring down my back, hear the voices in phrases I could only understand in bits and pieces.

But what I remember most is Kenneth beside me, serving God, praying for the people, hands raised in worship. We've done much together: raised two wonderful children, built a house, gone on vacations. But nothing connects us spiritually quite like the moments when we are contending for the gospel side by side.

Today's biblical woman just like us is Priscilla. I've always been intrigued by her story and wanted to know more. How did you and Aquila meet? What was it like to be on the run from Rome? Did you enjoy tentmaking? How did you come to know Christ?

From what we do know in Scripture, Priscilla and Aquila served God together. She is never mentioned in the Bible apart from him. Surely, she had times on her own; but when it comes to work and service, they were one.

So, what can we learn from them about serving God well?

First, their home was not their own.

> "After this, Paul left Athens and went to Corinth. There he met a Jew named Aquila, a native of Pontus, who had recently come from Italy with his wife Priscilla, because Claudius had ordered all the Jews to leave Rome. Paul went to see them, and because he was a tentmaker as they were, he stayed and worked with them. Every Sabbath he reasoned in the synagogue, trying to persuade Jews and Greeks" (Acts 18:1-4).

When Paul arrived in Corinth, he met Aquila, who was a tentmaker. Because Paul also was trained in that skill, he worked with them. But don't miss that he also stayed with them.

They opened their home to the missionary, giving him both a place to sleep, eat, and be refreshed and a place to work with his hands, to make a living, and to interact in the marketplace, thus making relationships and furthering his missionary work.

Sometimes we are willing to serve God in the public space, but we are not willing to open our homes. Priscilla and Aquila, however, knew their home was not their own. They not only opened it to host a missionary; they later planted a church at their home in Ephesus.

> "The churches in the province of Asia send you greetings. Aquila and Priscilla greet you warmly in the Lord, and so does the church that meets at their house" (1 Corinthians 16:19).

This couple served God side by side, contending for the gospel even at the cost of their own privacy and comfort. They considered their home belonged to God and offered it for the early Christians as a place of worship and discipleship in the body of Christ.

Second, their faith was not their own.

Priscilla and Aquila did not keep their faith to themselves. They were willing to share their understanding of the Word of God with others, no matter the cost.

> "Meanwhile a Jew named Apollos, a native of Alexandria, came to Ephesus. He was a learned man, with a thorough

knowledge of the Scriptures. He had been instructed in the way of the Lord, and he spoke with great fervor and taught about Jesus accurately, though he knew only the baptism of John. He began to speak boldly in the synagogue. When Priscilla and Aquila heard him, they invited him to their home and explained to him the way of God more accurately" (Acts 18:24-26).

This passage is one about which I would love to ask many questions one day! What seems clear, though, is that Apollos knew who Jesus was through the preaching of John the Baptist. He knew that Jesus was the fulfillment of the Old Testament prophecies.

John's baptism was one of repentance. But Jesus taught of the baptism in His name that is the result of faith in Him and His finished work on the cross (Matthew 28:19). Apparently, Apollos spoke the truth about Jesus, but didn't understand that one must express faith in Jesus in order to be saved.

When Priscilla and Aquila heard him speak, they recognized this truth. Rather than call him out publicly or humiliate him, they took him home and explained the truth. I'm sure they did it with much grace and love because Apollos went on to help others as a result of their ministry to him (Acts 18:27-28). What a testimony of the faith, grace, and sacrifice of this couple who served God together as one!

Third, their lives were not their own.

Although Priscilla and Aquila had both a home and a business in Corinth, they packed their bags and followed Paul when he left there to go to Ephesus. They left everything behind to follow God.

"Paul stayed on in Corinth for some time, Then he left the brothers and sailed for Syria, accompanied by Priscilla and Aquila" (Acts 18:18).

Wouldn't you love to have such an eternal perspective that the things of this world couldn't hold you back from wherever God leads? God may be calling us to leave a paying job in order to stay home with our kids, but we fear the loss of income and our current way of life. God may be calling us to step out in ministry, but we know we would have to give up much of our time or security to do so.

God may even be calling us to leave behind everything we know and follow Him into the unknown. And it's scary. Do we consider our lives our own? Or do we believe that He is ultimately in control of our lives anyway, so we may as well follow where He leads?

It may not be comfortable. It may even not be safe. I have a feeling that whenever we hear this next story one day in heaven, we may find out just how uncomfortable and risky this life chosen by Priscilla and Aquila really was.

"Greet Priscilla and Aquila, my fellow workers in Christ Jesus. They risked their lives for me. Not only I but all the churches of the Gentiles are grateful to them" (Romans 16:3-4).

The Bible gives us no more information about what happened. Apparently, it was well-known among the churches because they were all grateful for their sacrifice. Whatever happened, this Christian couple was willing to stick their necks out for Paul at the risk of death. This witness of God through His servants Priscilla and Aquila is one I will be meditating on for a while.

I'll be asking myself these questions:

Do I consider my home my own possession that I worked for and therefore can use as I see fit? The early church didn't.

> "All the believers were one in heart and mind. No one claimed that any of his possessions were his own, but they shared everything they had" (Acts 4:32).

Do I consider my faith my own personal business between me and God? Paul didn't as he demonstrated with his life and also in this letter to Philemon.

> "I pray you may be active in sharing your faith, so that you will have a full understanding of every good thing we have in Christ" (Philemon 1:6).

Do I consider my life my own to do with as I please?

> "Do you not know that your body is a temple of the Holy Spirit, who is in you, whom you have received from God? You are not your own; you were bought with a price. Therefore honor God with your body" (1 Corinthians 6:19-20).

This passage comes in the context of sexual sin, but the principle is the same: We are not our own. When we accept Jesus' payment on the cross for our sins, we are acknowledging that we were bought with His blood. Our lives belong to God.

I don't know about you, but Priscilla and Aquila's testimony is such an encouragement to me. Whether you have a spouse to serve alongside you in ministry, or like Paul, you serve with the Lord at your side, you can consider that your home, you faith, and your life belong to Him.

Together, let's serve Him well and be the example of sacrifice and faith that will bring Him glory and proclaim His kingdom throughout our world.

Even if He calls us to leave behind all we know to follow Him. It'll be worth it.

THE SEARCH FOR TRUTH

IN A WORLD OF LIES

WOMEN WHO STUDY THE WORD

———————— ⟨∽⟩ ————————

Do you consider yourself a student of God's Word?

The English word *disciple* comes from the Greek word *mathetes*, meaning "disciple, student, follower; a committed learner and follower." [11]

Sometimes we shy away from the word *disciple* (because it sounds too much like discipline) or the word *student* (because it sounds too much like school), but our hearts should be drawn to know and understand God's Word.

> "Do good to your servant according to your word, O LORD. Teach me knowledge and good judgment, for I believe in your commands" (Psalm 119:65-66).

Women in Jesus' day were not allowed to go to school or learn under rabbis. They were considered unable to learn or understand the Torah, and so they were taught to take care of the home.

But Jesus threw those traditions out the window. He had many women followers (Luke 8:1-3), and He taught women, considering them capable of learning and understanding His truth (Luke 10:38-

42). Jesus affirmed women's thirst for truth and encouraged their role as disciples.

Our roles as wives, mothers, and homemakers does not exclude our role as students of the Word. I love being a wife and mother (most days). I love taking care of our home, providing meals (okay, I don't really love cooking, but I do enjoy choosing healthy foods for our family!), and I like decorating our space to make it cozy and inviting.

I also enjoyed many years of teaching and working outside the home. But I have really loved the opportunity to sit at Jesus' feet as a student, to listen to His Word being preached, to study the Word for myself, to search out its meaning, and to seek to apply it in my life.

We don't have to wait for others to spoon-feed us the Bible. And as influencers in our homes, we need to know and understand God's truth so we can teach our children (Deuteronomy 6:4-9). I'll admit, there are areas of the Bible that are difficult to understand and that can cause confusion. But with a few principles to guide us, we can learn to be students of the Word.

First, our problem is often not one of misunderstanding, but of failing to apply the clear directives God gives us. When we get confused about something, we can always stop and think of all the truths of God's Word that are clear, and focus on obedience to them.

> "This is love for God: to obey his commands. And his commands are not burdensome, for everyone born of God

overcomes the world. This is the victory that has overcome the world, even our faith" (1 John 5:3-4).

We obey by faith, even when we don't always understand; so we shouldn't use lack of understanding as an excuse not to obey what we do know.

Second, we can do word studies, read commentaries, and study cross-references to see what other related verses say about a difficult passage.

Remember to let Scripture interpret Scripture. In other words, we should always compare the passage we are studying to the whole counsel of the Word. God's Word will never contradict itself, so what we believe a Scripture is saying should be in line with the rest of the Bible.

> "Do your best to present yourself to God as one approved, a workman who does not need to be ashamed and who correctly handles the word of truth" (2 Timothy 2:15).

Third, we can ask our pastor or someone we trust with the Word to guide us in areas of confusion. Remember to hold every opinion up to the whole counsel of the Word. Just because something sounds good doesn't mean it is correct. Again, it should align with the rest of Scripture.

> "If anyone teaches false doctrines and does not agree to the sound instruction of our Lord Jesus Christ and to godly teaching, he is conceited and understands nothing" (1 Timothy 6:3-4a).

Fourth, we can learn how to interpret the Bible ourselves—something that doesn't require a seminary degree to do. Some good books are Jen Wilkin's *Women of the Word* and Fee and Stuart's *How to Read the Bible for All Its Worth*.

We can learn how to determine a good translation, how to study Scripture within context, and how to apply what we learn to our daily lives.

Fifth, we can pray and ask the Holy Spirit for wisdom and understanding of God's Word. He inspired the Word of God, and He can teach us as we study and apply these principles of sound interpretation. We must be careful, however, that we do not neglect one for the other. We need both the leading of the Spirit and sound interpretation.

> "We have not received the spirit of the world but the Spirit who is from God, that we may understand what God has freely given us" (1 Corinthians 2:12).

And last, remember there are some things we will not know this side of eternity.

> "'For my thoughts are not your thoughts, neither are your ways my ways,' declares the Lord. 'As the heavens are higher than the earth, so are my ways higher than your ways and my thoughts than your thoughts'" (Isaiah 55:8-9).

We can wrestle all day long with some issues, but many of them have been debated for centuries and will continue to be. The important thing is that we are walking with God and seeking to obey Him in the things we do understand.

So, do you consider yourself to be a disciple of Christ? We live in a time in which we as women have great opportunity and resources to be students of the Word. So, what are you waiting for? Get out that Bible, and dig in!

If you are interested in learning more about how to study the Bible, join our Facebook group, *Growing Your Faith*, where we share tools and teaching videos to help you grow.

WOMEN WHO GROW

I heard someone say recently that you can be a 25-year Christian, or you can be a one-year-old Christian for 25 years. The Bible actually has much to say about spiritual maturity and the call to grow in the Lord. One reason our churches don't grow is because of a lack of spiritual maturity.

When we first come to Jesus, we are spiritual babies. At my former church, we had a "baby" shower every time there was a baptism. When someone committed his life to the Lord, we celebrated the new life with a party and gifts.

Those gifts included a Bible, devotions, journals, even Christian music—things that would help the new believer surround himself with the things of the kingdom, rather than the world.

Just as a physical baby needs nourishment to survive, a new Christian needs a steady diet of the Word, prayer, and fellowship with other Christians. As a baby grows into a toddler and must be guided as he learns to walk, we need others to show us how to walk with the Lord.

In fact, Paul shared this as his prayer for the Colossians:

"And we pray this in order that you may live a life worthy of the Lord and may please him in every way: bearing fruit in every good work, growing in the knowledge of God, and being strengthened with all power according to his glorious might so that you may have great endurance and patience" (1:10-11).

Peter shared this:

"But grow in the grace and knowledge of our Lord and Savior Jesus Christ" (2 Peter 3:18).

If a baby doesn't grow, he will be diagnosed with "failure to thrive," which left untreated, leads to death. The same is true of us spiritually. If we are not thriving, our fire for the Lord will die out and we will be useless in God's kingdom.

So how do we know if we need to grow up? The Bible gives us some signs of what spiritual immaturity looks like:

First, immature Christians don't crave the word.

"Like newborn babies, crave pure spiritual milk, so that by it you may grow up in your salvation, now that you have tasted that the Lord is good" (1 Peter 2:2-3).

You see, Peter is saying when you first become a believer, you ought to crave the "milk" of the Word, just like a little baby craves its mama's milk. But notice he says that by that Word, we should grow up in our salvation. So we aren't supposed to stay on the milk forever.

The writer of Hebrews describes the problem of not growing in the Word:

> "We have much to say about this, but it is hard to explain because you are slow to learn. In fact, though by this time you ought to be teachers, you need someone to teach you the elementary truths of God's Word all over again. You need milk, not solid food! Anyone who lives on milk, being still an infant, is not acquainted with the teaching about righteousness. But solid food is for the mature, who by constant use have trained themselves to distinguish good from evil" (Hebrews 5:11-14).

Well, he doesn't really hold back, now, does he?

God is saying to us that He wants to take us to a higher place in Him, but we can't comprehend it because we're like a 10-year-old sucking on a bottle. By this time, some of us should be the big sister, feeding another baby, discipling and encouraging others in the faith. But we still haven't trained ourselves in the Word.

The mature Christian continues to crave the Word so that she is able to grow from the milk to the meat.

Second, immature Christians still love the world.

> "Brothers, I could not address you as spiritual but as worldly—mere infants in Christ. I gave you milk, not solid food, for you were not yet ready for it. Indeed, you are still not ready. You are still worldy. For since there is jealousy and quarreling among you, are you not worldly?" (1 Corinthians 3:1-3a).

Is there anything more ungodly than Christians who have been in church for years, caught up in jealousy and quarreling? Paul says that is a mark of worldliness—spiritual immaturity. If they had been growing in the Word, they would be convicted of their sin and seeking to turn away from it. That's what a mature Christian does.

Worldly Christians are those who still have a me-first attitude. They want things their way, and they don't care whom they hurt to get it. But that's not God's way.

God wants to address us spiritually, reveal new truth to us, deliver us from sin and bad habits, and grow us into His image. But many of us are still crawling around in the same stinking diaper we were wearing last year—still holding onto bitterness, jealousy, unforgiveness, pride, and selfishness. Worldly.

The mature Christian loves the things of God more than the things of the world.

Third, immature Christians don't want to work.

> "It was he who gave some to be apostles, some to be prophets, some to be evangelists, and some to be pastors and teachers, to prepare God's people for works of service, so that the body of Christ may be built up until we come to unity in the faith and in the knowledge of the Son of God and become mature, attaining to the whole measure of the fullness of Christ" (Ephesians 4:12-13).

Bless our pastors, they are trying to prepare us for works of service, but they spend most of their time plugging in our pacifiers. Our churches aren't building the kingdom because of the lack of unity, faith, and knowledge. We need to grow up.

> "Then we will no longer be infants, tossed back and forth by the waves, blown here and there by every wind of teaching and by the cunning and craftiness of men in their deceitful scheming. Instead, speaking the truth in love, we will in all things grow up into him who is the head, that is, Christ. From him the whole body, joined and held together by every supporting ligament, grows and builds itself up in love, as each part does its work" (Ephesians 4:14-16).

When we grow up, we get to work. We stop wasting time on meaningless activities, and we get focused on the mission. We stop striving to get our way about everything, and we start seeking to build others up. We start working together in unity, because regardless of our own opinion, we have a common mission that outweighs our wants.

When we grow up, we stop gossiping and quarreling and being jealous of one another. We value and seek peace over personal opinions. We seek to give more than we receive. We look for other people to be kind and generous to.

When we grow up, we crave the meat of the Word. We long for quiet time, Bible study, and church. We can't wait to see what God is up to next in our lives, because we know we are on a great adventure with Him to build His kingdom on earth.

And best of all, we start caring for some other babies by holding and feeding and supporting them while we watch them learn to walk and grow up in Him.

Want one more sign that we might need to grow up?

If we thought this message was for someone else.

WOMEN WHO ABIDE IN JESUS

I've never been much for wearing hats. Don't get me wrong; I like hats. They look great on other people. Me—not so much. But truthfully, I wear a lot of hats. I bet you do, too.

As women, we often serve many roles: wife, mother, daughter, sister, friend, co-worker, boss, church worker, home designer, chauffeur, chef, coach, homework assistant, shall I continue? How can we as women function in all these capacities in a manner that is fruitful and productive?

> "I am the vine; you are the branches. If a man remains in me and I in him, he will bear much fruit; apart from me you can do nothing" (John 15:5).

We can find the word *remain* in John 15 eleven times! The Greek word used here is *meno*, which means "to stay, remain, live, dwell, abide; to be in a state that begins and continues."[12]

In other words, apart from Jesus, we can't live a fruitful life. We must remain in Him, and that means we need to "begin and continue" our day with Him. We need to begin our day with Jesus.

We can't remain somewhere we haven't first been. Our day must begin with the Lord. If you are a mom of littles, finding space in the mornings can be extra difficult, but I encourage you to find a few minutes to at least read a short devotional.

> "Very early in the morning while it was still dark, Jesus got up, left the house and went to a solitary place, where he prayed" (Mark 1:35).

Even Jesus needed to start His day with the Father, and so do we. Starting our day with Jesus gives us the opportunity for a fresh start every single day—a chance to come clean of any sin in our lives and commit a new day to Him for His glory.

> "Because of the LORD's great love we are not consumed, for his compassions never fail. They are new every morning; great is your faithfulness" (Lamentations 3:22-23).

We can come to Him with our needs and petitions, letting go of anxiety and fear.

> "In the morning, O LORD, you hear my voice; in the morning I lay my requests before you and wait in expectation" (Psalm 5:3).

I know we are not all morning people, and there's no condemnation for those who just can't find time in the mornings; but I do know from experience that any sacrifice we make for Him is worth it. We may need to get up fifteen minutes earlier, seek Him during our kids' naptime, or make our lunch hour our quiet time.

Remember, we can do nothing without Him—not a few things or some things. No thing. If we want to be fruitful and productive in our day, we need to begin with Jesus.

We also need to continue in Christ.

Remember the Greek word for *remain* means to begin and continue in something. If we are to remain in Him, we will have to continue to keep our minds on Jesus throughout the day.

> "Those who live according to the sinful nature have their minds set on what that nature desires; but those who live in accordance with the Spirit have their minds set on what the Spirit desires" (Romans 8:5).

With all the many responsibilities we carry each day, how can we practically live out this mandate to keep our minds "set on what the Spirit desires"? I believe three elements are key to a mind set on the Spirit: the Word, obedience, and faith.

First, we have to spend time in the Word to know what is pleasing to the Spirit of God.

> "I have hidden your word in my heart that I might not sin against you" (Psalm 119:11).

As we study the Word through our daily quiet time, Bible study, and sermons, we will have a mind that is being renewed daily from our old way of thinking to the mind of Christ.

> "Do not conform any longer to the pattern of this world, but be transformed by the renewing of your mind" (Romans 12:2a).

162

Second, we must obey what we learn from God's truth.

> "Do not merely listen to the word, and so deceive yourselves. Do what it says" (James 1:22).

Jesus told His disciples that if they would listen to His Words and "put them into practice," they would be building their lives on a solid foundation that would withstand the storms of life (Matthew 7:24-27).

Third, we need faith to believe that God will be with us and equip us for whatever we face each day. The stress of daily responsibilities and the pull of the world's temptation will quickly wear us out if we don't lean by faith on Him.

> "We live by faith, not by sight" (2 Corinthians 5:7).

We have to trust that He is in us, with us, and working in our lives to accomplish His divine purposes. As we learn to walk with Him by faith, we will grow in understanding of His ways and awareness of His presence.

Remaining in Jesus throughout the day means that we continue to walk in His Word with faith and obedience, living moment by moment in the truths His Word reveals.

We were chosen and appointed to bear fruit.

> "You did not choose me, but I chose you and appointed you to go and bear fruit—fruit that will last" (John 15:16).

No matter how many hats we are juggling, our daily goal is to bear fruit—to live a life that bears witness to the love, grace, and truth of Jesus Christ. Whether we are building a family, a career, a ministry, or a business, our primary role is to build the Kingdom.

We can't be on mission with God unless we are starting each day with Jesus and remaining with Him as we go. Folding laundry, changing diapers, caring for an elderly parent, singing in the choir, growing a business, loving our families, or leading a small group— none of it will bear fruit apart from Him; but all of it can be done with a spirit of love, joy, and peace, testifying to the goodness of our God.

So, go ahead and wear all those hats today, but remember to sit at His feet a little while first. Then you will have the power you need to wear them well.

WHAT MAMAS TEACH US
ABOUT THE GOSPEL

Mothers have a special place in God's heart. Of all the ways God could have chosen to insert Himself into our world, He chose to do so through a mother. And His mother was important to Him. So much so, that when He was suffering the torture of the cross in extreme agony, He made provision for her to be cared for by his best friend.

> "When Jesus saw his mother there, and the disciple whom he loved, standing nearby, he said to his mother, 'Dear woman, here is your son,' and to the disciple, 'Here is your mother.' From that time on, this disciple took her into his home" (John 19:26-27).

I'm not sure how much Jesus just "knew" because He was God in the flesh, but I'm sure Mary still taught Him many things. He had to grow, to be nurtured, to learn how to walk, to put on his sandals.

The same Holy Spirit who lived in Jesus inspired these words written through Solomon:

> "Listen, my son, to your father's instruction and do not forsake your mother's teaching" (Proverbs 1:8).

I think mothers actually teach us a lot about the gospel. Through the gentleness, comfort, and instruction of our mothers we see the blueprint for sharing Jesus with those around us.

Be gentle.

> "As apostles of Christ we could have been a burden to you, but we were gentle among you, like a mother caring for her little children. We loved you so much that we were delighted to share with you not only the gospel of God but our lives as well, because you had become so dear to us" (1 Thessalonians 2:6b-8).

Paul is saying that as apostles, they had the right to seek support from the church in their efforts to spread the gospel, but they were motivated not by greed but by love.

Sometimes sharing the gospel can become about what we can get out of it—building our church or ministry, seeing our loved ones make better choices that impact us—to the point that we are no longer motivated by love but by our own selfish interests. Our hearts will then be reflected in our actions, words, and even our countenance.

A mother's gentleness and care toward her babies can be a great example of how we should share "not only the gospel of God but our lives as well."

Show comfort.

> "As a mother comforts a child, so will I comfort you" (Jeremiah 66:13).

Another great example from moms is found in how they comfort a child. If we are hurt, wounded, sad, or afraid, we need our mamas to be there for us. I am almost fifty years old, but when I'm sick or hurting, I still want my mama.

Because God comforts us in this way, we are called to bring comfort to those around us. In sharing the gospel, we will often find that those who are living in darkness are also in pain. They need the truth of the gospel—the Light of Jesus—to bring them out of darkness.

But they also need the comfort of someone caring enough to give them a hug or hold their hand.

Sharing the gospel is more than just telling someone how to be saved. We also need to demonstrate the love of Jesus in their lives so they can see His love through us.

> "Praise be to the God and Father of our Lord Jesus Christ, the Father of compassion and the God of all comfort, who comforts us in all our troubles, so that we can comfort those in any trouble with the comfort we ourselves have received from God" (2 Corinthians 1:3-4).

A mother's comforting presence, prayers, and touch are sometimes exactly what a lost person needs to show her the truth of who God really is.

But moms aren't all roses and sunshine.

Correct when necessary.

Sometimes mamas have to correct, instruct, and rebuke. Godly mothers will have a standard of right and wrong by which they expect their children to abide. When their kids cross that line, mamas know how to bring them back.

> "The rod of correction imparts wisdom, but a child left to himself disgraces his mother" (Proverbs 29:15).

I know there is much controversy over the use of spanking as a means of discipline because there are parents who cross the line into abuse. But I do believe the idea here in this Proverb is that children have to be corrected. The Hebrew word translated *rod* actually means branch. I got a few switches in my day!

Regardless, the point here is that a mother who wants to impart wisdom to her child rather than suffer disgrace will correct her child. Isn't that a beautiful picture of the gospel?

We were once lost in sin on a path that leads to hell. Someone came along beside us and shared the truth of God's Word—the standard of right and wrong. We acknowledged that we are sinners and sought forgiveness through Jesus Christ.

Now, as we grow, we need faithful sisters in our lives who will speak truth and correct us when we go astray.

> "Brothers, if someone is caught in a sin, you who are spiritual should restore him gently" (Galatians 6:1).

Just as a loving mother will correct her child and bring him back into a right relationship, we are to offer loving, gentle correction to our brothers and sisters, especially those who are young Christians and just beginning to grow in their faith.

One of my favorite Bible passages describes how the love of God has been passed down from mother to child for generations.

> "I have been reminded of your sincere faith, which first lived in your grandmother Lois and in your mother Eunice and, I am persuaded, now lives in you also" (2 Timothy 1:5).

Here we find Lois, who first became a believer in Christ. She shared the gospel with her daughter Eunice because she loved her. Eunice then shared the gospel with Timothy, to whom Paul was writing. Mamas sharing the gospel with their littles—here we find the perfect motivation for sharing the love of Jesus with others: Because we love them!

There's nothing quite like the love of a mother for a child. Until we parent someone else, we can never understand the depth of love and passion that we can have for another. And God calls us to love the lost with that very same passion.

Years ago, while my children were at vacation Bible school, a storm came up that was much like a tornado (I thought it was!) The sky turned black, then completely white from the heavy rain. It turned out to be straight-line winds, but the storm did much damage to our back porch.

As soon as the roaring stopped and I saw the destruction, I ran outside to the car to go check on my kids. But our basketball goal had been knocked across our driveway behind my car. The goal is the type that has water in the base to hold it down. Before that day, I had never had the strength to move that basketball goal even an inch.

That day, I picked it up and moved the entire goal from behind my car to get to my children. I think it could have been a tank, and it still would have moved. There's a strength and a fierce passion in a mother's heart that will move mountains to save her children.

What about us?

Will we go to any length—moving mountains if necessary—to share the love and truth of the gospel with others? Are we desperate to rescue them from hell so they can enjoy a life of freedom, joy, and peace?

Mamas have a lot to teach us. Whether you have biological children or spiritual children, let's all seek to model a mama's love to those around us. Some have never known the love of God or the love of a mother.

We can show them both.

WOMEN WHO KNOW
HOW TO DRESS

I'm not really a girly-girl. Never have been. I hate to shop, and it takes me forever to pick out something to wear when I have to be dressed up. If I could live the rest of my life in jeans, t-shirts, and flip flops, I would. But sometimes I have to dress up for special occasions. When I do, I put on and take off, put on and take off, put on and take off. It's exhausting.

God calls us to put on and take off some things as well. And if we do it right, it won't be tiresome; it'll be awesome.

"The night is nearly over; the day is almost here. So let us put aside the deeds of darkness and put on the armor of light. Let us behave decently, as in the daytime, not in orgies and drunkenness, not in sexual immorality and debauchery, not in dissension and jealousy. Rather clothe yourselves with the Lord Jesus Christ, and do not think about how to gratify the desires of the sinful nature" (Romans 13:12-14).

Paul is saying that now that the death and resurrection of Jesus have taken place, we are closer to the time of His return, and we need to act like it. We need to take off sinful behavior and put on Jesus by changing the way we think.

The thing about finding something to wear is that we get to choose. When we're trying on outfits before we go somewhere, we have to make a choice about what to wear—pants or skirt, prints or solids, sandals or pumps. The closer it gets to our time to leave, the more panicked we become, especially if we can't find just the right accessory or outfit that we feel good in.

We should be just as concerned about the way we live our lives the closer we get to judgment day. The Bible says we will give an account before God for every careless word we've spoken (Matthew 12:36). We need to choose to put on Christ every day.

> "You are all sons of God through faith in Christ Jesus, for all of you who were baptized into Christ have clothed yourselves with Christ" (Galatians 3:26-27).

This Scripture tells me that sometimes we are already wearing the right thing, we just don't know it. We need to submit to the leading of the Holy Spirit within us and walk in that Spirit. But that old sinful nature keeps creeping in with the wrong attitudes. We feel like we have to dress to impress or try to be something that we're not. We try to camouflage those areas we feel aren't good enough instead of just letting God make it into something new.

> "You were taught with regard to your former way of life, to put off your old self, which is being corrupted by its deceitful desires; to be made new in the attitude of your minds; and to put on the new self, created to be like God in true righteousness and holiness" (Ephesians 4:22-24).

We must believe by faith that God does the work of changing us from the inside out and then make the choice to lay aside those old patterns of thinking and bad habits. Then we can walk in the newness of life He died to give us.

Paul goes on to tell us in this passage that we need to put off falsehood and "get rid of all bitterness, rage and anger, brawling and slander, along with every form of malice" (4:25, 31). He tells us to instead be "kind and compassionate to one another, forgiving each other" (32).

You see, even though we have been changed by God, those old sinful patterns and ways of the world are sometimes hard to let go of. We also have an enemy who will constantly bombard our minds with thoughts that lead us astray. That's why we have to be reminded to take off and put on.

One of the most important pieces of our wardrobe is the armor of God. Paul tells us that some of it we already have, we just need to stand firm in it:

> "Stand firm them, with the belt of truth buckled around your waist, with the breastplate of righteousness in place, and with your feet fitted with the readiness that comes from the gospel of peace" (Ephesians 6:14-15).

We already have the truth: Jesus is the way, the truth, and the life (John 14:6). We already have righteousness. We are the righteousness of God in Christ Jesus (2 Corinthians 5:21). And we can stand on the gospel of peace because it is by this gospel that we are saved (1 Corinthians 15:2). We just need to "stand firm" in these truths.

But then we have some accessories to add before we walk out the door:

> "In addition to all this, take up the shield of faith, with which you can extinguish all the flaming arrows of the evil one. Take the helmet of salvation and the sword of the Spirit, which is the word of God" (Ephesians 6:16-17).

These pieces require us to take them up. In other words, we have to choose each day to walk in faith, to hope in our salvation, and to speak the Word of God over our lives.

Just as we choose each day what we will wear around the house, to work, to church, or to run errands, we must choose how we will act towards our family, our coworkers, our church family, and in our community.

> "Therefore as God's chosen people, holy and dearly loved, clothe yourselves with compassion, kindness, humility, gentleness, and patience. Bear with one another and forgive whatever grievances you may have against one another. Forgive as the Lord forgave you. And over all these virtues, put on love, which binds them all together in perfect unity" (Colossians 3:12-14).

We will never be more beautiful than when we are clothed in God's character. We will be attractive to others. We'll have confidence in our witness. And we will be at peace with ourselves and with God.

So, the next time you're like me standing in front of the mirror, running out of time to get somewhere, and still not happy with what you have to wear, just remember this Word:

> "Your beauty should not come from outward adornment, such as braided hair and the wearing of jewelry and fine clothes. Instead, it should be that of your inner self, the unfading beauty of a gentle and quiet spirit, which is of great worth in God's sight. For this is the way the holy women of the past who put their hope in God used to make themselves beautiful" (1 Peter 3:3-5).

I love this passage, because even the Bible acknowledges that as women, we want to feel beautiful. And there's nothing wrong with that. We can fix our hair and wear jewelry and nice clothes. Peter is saying just don't get all wrapped up in that, because what makes you beautiful is what's on the inside shining through.

So choose to get dressed each day in the character of Christ. You already have Him in you. Just choose to live it and walk on out the door.

WOMEN WHO
BUILD THEIR HOMES
ON THE ROCK

———————— ⟨∽⟩ ————————

What foundation are you building on?

> "Wisdom has built her house; she has hewn out its seven
> pillars. She has prepared her meat and mixed her wine; she has
> also set her table" (Proverbs 9:1-2).

Wisdom is personified in these passages as a woman who builds
her house and sets her table. She then calls out an invitation for
those who are simple to come to her house and join her for a meal.

Wisdom has built her house. I like to think of this as a woman who
takes the time to think about the materials with which she is
building. Jesus had something to say about how we build.

> "I will show you what he is like who comes to me and hears
> my words and puts them into practice. He is like a man
> building a house, who dug down deep and laid the foundation
> on rock. When a flood came, the torrent struck that house but
> could not shake it, because it was well built" (Luke 6:47-48).

We can know what the Word says, but if we do not put it into
practice, we are not building a house—we're just playing in the
sand.

Let's build our homes on the Rock.

> "Unless the Lord builds the house, its builders labor in vain" (Psalm 127:1).

We need to build on the Rock of our salvation, which is Jesus Christ. If we live a life that acknowledges God as only *part* of our lives, we are in trouble. When Jesus is the foundation of the life we are building, He is not part of our lives. He *is* our life.

Wisdom also builds with seven pillars. Seven is the number of completion in the Bible, so let's look at seven qualities of wisdom according to James.

Let's frame our homes with wisdom.

> "But the wisdom that comes from heaven is first of all pure; then peace-loving, considerate, submissive, full of mercy and good fruit, impartial, and sincere. Peacemakers who sow in peace raise a harvest of righteousness" (James 3:17-18).

Imagine if we built our lives and our homes on the foundation of the Word of God and our salvation, and then we framed it in with purity, peace, consideration, submission, mercy and good fruit, impartiality, and sincerity. Now, that's a house worth living in. And that's a home worth inviting others to.

But Wisdom does one more thing. She sets a table. She prepares the meat and mixes the wine. The meat and wine remind me of the blood of the covenant and the meat of God's Word.

As women of wisdom, we can invite others to the table to share the gospel of grace available by faith in the blood of Christ. We can disciple other women in the truth of God's Word.

Let's invite others to the table. But know that Folly sends out invitations, too.

> "The woman Folly is loud; she is undisciplined and without knowledge. She sits at the door of her house, on a seat at the highest point of the city, calling out to those who pass by, who go straight on their way. 'Let all who are simple come in here!' she says to those who lack judgment" (Proverbs 9:13-16).

Folly is an attention-seeker; she has to be the loudest voice. She may be popular, but she is leading others to destruction.

> "But little do they know that the dead are there, that her guests are in the depths of the grave" (Proverbs 9:18).

Folly hasn't even set a table, because what she has to offer is not worthy of the table.

> "'Stolen water is sweet; food eaten in secret is delicious!'" (Proverbs 9:17).

It may seem that what she has to offer is delicious—sin is enticing. But the truth is that what is done in secret will eventually be revealed. Sin has consequences that are not so pleasant.

These passages in Proverbs are written to warn us to follow the ways of wisdom and not folly. But I think they also serve as instructions to us as women. Which woman do we want to be? We can be the attention-seeker—loud and undisciplined, manipulative, and leading others astray. Or we can be the voice of wisdom and truth to those around us—to our families, friends, co-workers, and neighbors.

Let's be women of wisdom. Let's build a home on the foundation of truth with the walls of wisdom. Let's set a table with food that will endure and drink that will quench every thirst. Let's invite others to the home we have built and the table we have set and offer them life.

Our homes can become a place to share the gospel. Our table can be a place to disciple someone. So, how about it? Do you know someone, young or old, who needs an invitation?

"Come, eat my food and drink the wine I have mixed. Leave your simple ways and you will live" (Proverbs 9:6).

The house and table of wisdom lead to life.

So what are you building, and whom have you invited?

HUNGRY FOR TRUTH: THE WOMEN OF BEREA

I ran into a lady recently who invited me to speak at her book club. I asked her what book they were reading. Her response?

"Oh, we don't read."

"You have a book club, but you don't read? So...what do you do?"

She smiled warmly. "We just love to socialize."

I thought it was great. Who says women need a reason to socialize anyway? If we want to gather with friends to eat and talk, awesome!

But later it occurred to me that's how many people view the church—kind of like a club for socializing, but we need an excuse, so we call it "God." Oh, we aren't all that interested in what He has to say, but He gives us a great excuse for our gathering.

The Bereans were cut from a different cloth, though.

On Paul's second missionary journey, he and Silas traveled from Thessalonica to Berea, both cities in Macedonia. As they arrived in Berea and began preaching at the synagogue, they noticed a different response.

"Now the Bereans were of more noble character than the Thessalonians, for they received the message with great eagerness and examined the Scriptures every day to see if what Paul said was true. Many of the Jews believed, as did also a number of prominent Greek women and men" (Acts 17:11-12).

These men and women were hungry for truth. They didn't show up just for coffee and social hour. Sure, they may have enjoyed time together outside of church. But they came to the synagogue for truth. The Bereans didn't go to church for the music, the preacher, or the programs. They went because they wanted to encounter the truth of God's Word. They were hungry to understand God and His ways.

"Jesus answered, 'It is written: "Man does not live on bread alone, but on every word that comes from the mouth of God"'" (Matthew 4:4).

The Bereans showed up with one agenda: to hear the message. Our Berean believers didn't sit back with a "bless-me-if-you-can attitude." They didn't sit in a pew, read the Bible verses from the screen, shake a few hands, and go home. No, these guys were hungry for truth. They were the type who bring their Bibles, take notes, listen attentively, and think of questions to ask later.

"Pay attention and listen to the sayings of the wise; apply your heart to what I teach" (Proverbs 22:17).

The Bereans weren't content to just take the word of any teaching that came along. They were determined to search the Bible for themselves, because they were hungry for truth, not just fellowship.

The Bible gives us many warnings about false teachers. The reason so many people get led astray by doctrines and philosophies contrary to Scripture is because they don't search the Scriptures for themselves.

> "Dear friends, do not believe every spirit, but test the spirits to see whether they are from God, because many false prophets have gone out into the world" (1 John 4:1).

Many are content to sit back and let somebody else feed them, but unless they are willing to examine the food they are being served, they are in danger of being poisoned. Luke (the writer of Acts) tells us that these Bereans were of "more noble character" than the Thessalonians. To be of more noble character means they were excellent in their way of being and doing.

This excellence means that they weren't searching the Scriptures to find fault in the speaker, they were searching to find truth. They confirmed that what Paul was saying lined up with the Scriptures. They compared to see that he wasn't taking verses out of context. These believers were hungry for truth.

And as they encountered truth, they believed. They believed the message Paul shared with them—that Jesus was the Messiah, that He suffered and was raised to life, that He truly was the Christ who had come to save them—Jew and Gentile, male and female alike.

What about us? Are we hungry for truth or just starved for attention? Do we go to church to socialize, or do we expect to experience God? Are we eager to receive the Word, or are we watching the clock and thinking about what we will eat for lunch?

I hear so many people who leave a church because they "aren't being fed" or they "didn't like the preacher's style." My heart breaks when I hear that because there are persecuted believers in other nations who would love to have the opportunity we have to sit in a warm (or cool) building and hear someone expound on the Scriptures.

They would be thrilled to have a complete Bible to read and study for themselves. They would be eager to receive the message of truth that we sometimes take for granted. As long as our pastor preaches the Word, we should have an eagerness to receive it. It's the Word of God! We don't go to church to feel good or be fed. We go to church to worship the Living God.

It's not about us. It's all about Jesus.

And you know my friend with the book club? Well, some of those ladies do love to read. Turns out their love for books has become contagious. What started as a ladies' group many years ago has now become a fellowship of warm hearts who share each other's lives and seek to do good in their community.

Passion is contagious.

So, let's be of more noble character and hungry for truth. Let's have a love for God's Word that inspires others. And let's seek to be the Church that God created us to be with a passion that is contagious.

After all, we can socialize any time. And, for that, we ladies don't even need an excuse.

NOT PERSUADED: BERNICE

I can still recall when I first understood the truth that God loved me enough to send His Son to die for me. I remember lifting my hands to the Father, tears streaming down my face, as I choked out words of surrender.

I didn't understand everything in that moment; in fact, it came after months of going to church, reading the Bible, and trying to wrap my head around what it truly means to follow Christ. But I knew enough. I understood that the words of a prayer uttered months earlier had not come from a heart of sincerity—they were spoken in hopes of satisfying the desires of someone else.

I understood that those months of trying to do the right thing and making a mess of it were the result of a spoken confession without an inward conversion. I also understood in that moment that the God I was trying to claim didn't need my good works. He wanted my heart. And after months of sitting under godly discipleship, worship, and the Word, I surrendered to the God who had revealed Himself to me.

So, my heart breaks when I encounter those who have heard the truth, maybe even been in church for a while, but they have never really given their lives to the One who loved and gave Himself for them.

One woman of the Bible whose story is both brief and heart-breaking is Bernice. We don't get many words in Scripture about her, but she too heard the truth, yet never surrendered her life. Bernice was the sister of Herod Agrippa II, and she had the privilege of hearing the first-hand testimony of the Apostle Paul.

Paul had been arrested in Ephesus after a mob accused him of desecrating the temple. Paul testified before the crowd, was jailed for his own protection, and eventually sent to the Roman governor, Felix. Paul testified that he had only gone to the temple to worship and present offerings, and that those who made the charges were not even present to accuse him. Felix had no reason to charge him, but left him under house arrest.

Two years went by, and eventually Festus succeeded Felix as governor. Because Paul as a Roman citizen had appealed to Caesar, Festus needed to send a letter explaining the charges against Paul, but he didn't know how to charge him.

So, he brought in King Agrippa and his sister Bernice because they would understand Jewish customs. As the Roman-appointed "kings" over Judea, the Herodian dynasty was not truly Jewish. But they ruled over the Jews for Rome and were acquainted with their ways.

Now, according to the Jewish historian Josephus, Bernice had been married at 13 and then widowed with two sons. She was suspected of having an incestuous relationship with Agrippa, so she married again to the king of Cilicia to silence the rumors but eventually left him to return to her brother.

At some point, Bernice became involved in a relationship with Emperor Vespasian's son Titus, but was "later ignored by him" for political reasons. She had a difficult life, to say the least. And now God had given her the opportunity to hear the gospel from the lips of Paul who had met Jesus on the road to Damascus.

> "The next day Agrippa and Bernice came with great pomp and entered the audience room with the high ranking officers and the leading men of the city" (Acts 25:1).

Festus explained the situation and then gave Paul the opportunity to speak.

> "So Paul motioned with his hand and began his defense: 'King Agrippa, I consider myself fortunate to stand before you today as I make my defense against all the accusations of the Jews, and especially so because you are well acquainted with all the Jewish customs and controversies. Therefore, I beg you to listen to me patiently" (Acts 26:1b-3).

Paul went on to give his testimony from the time he was a child, raised as a Pharisee, and putting his faith in the God of the Jews. He told of how he persecuted the followers of Jesus, casting votes to put them to death.

He then shared about his conversion experience on the road to Damascus when he met the Lord Jesus. Paul shared that he had only sought to be obedient to what God had called him to do:

preaching repentance of sins and salvation through Christ. He spoke of Christ's very words to him:

> """I will rescue you from your own people and from the Gentiles. I am sending you to them to open their eyes and turn them from darkness to light, and from the power of Satan to God, so that they may receive forgiveness of sins and a place among those who are sanctified by faith in me""" (Acts 26:17-18).

When Paul testified that Christ had fulfilled the OT prophets as the One who would proclaim light to the Gentiles, Festus accused Him of being insane.

> "I am not insane, most excellent Festus,' Paul replied. 'What I am saying is true and reasonable. The king is familiar with these things, and I can speak freely to him. I am convinced that none of this has escaped his notice, because it was not done in a corner. King Agrippa, do you believe the prophets? I know you do'" (Acts 26:25-27).

At this point, I am on the edge of my seat. I'm sure Bernice was, too. After all, the life, death, and resurrection of Jesus had not been done in a corner. They had heard about it. Now would they believe the testimony of one who had encountered the living Christ?

A God who could open eyes and turn darkness to light? The hope of being rescued from the power of Satan and receiving forgiveness of sins?

Surely this was the good news Bernice needed in her life. But now if Agrippa says he believes in the prophets, he would have to admit that all this about Jesus made sense. If he said no, he would be in trouble with the Jews.

> "Then Agrippa said to Paul, 'Do you think that in such a short time you can persuade me to be a Christian?'
>
> Paul replied, 'Short time or long—I pray God that not only you but all who are listening to me today may become what I am, except for these chains.'
>
> The king rose, and with him the governor and Bernice and those sitting with them. They left the room, and while talking with one another, they said, 'This man is not doing anything that deserves death or imprisonment'" (Acts 26:28-31).

Not persuaded by truth. That's the sad testimony of Bernice. We never hear of Bernice in Scripture again. In fact, she disappeared from the historical records as well, because the Roman emperors wanted to politically distance themselves from her.

Bernice is known historically as guilty, depraved, and shameless, but she had the opportunity to be known among such names as Lydia, Phoebe, and Priscilla. She was familiar with the ways of God, and she heard the truth of the gospel. But she walked away.

Bernice stands before us as an example of the hopelessness of life without Jesus. So many women all around us have heard the truth. They may even sit in the pews around you as I did for some time. Yet, they have never surrendered their lives to the Lord.

May we learn from Bernice's story to not take Christ's sacrifice for granted. May we share it boldly with those around us, praying that they may be persuaded to become a Christian, too.

And if you are like I was, and you have heard the truth but never understood the impact of Jesus' sacrifice for you personally, it's time to lift your hands in surrender to God.

Jesus has made a way for you to know Him. It's time to give up and let Him have His way in you. It doesn't matter what you've done or where you've been. He will take your guilt and shame and give you a life worth living.

How will you respond to truth?

DISCERNING TRUTH: DAMARIS

———————— ⌒ ————————

With the prevalence of social media and meme theology, we have become inundated with every form of philosophy and opinion—so much so, that often contradictory ideas can cause confusion and doubt, even among Christians.

Oh, the ideas have always abounded, we just weren't always so aware of them. And as my own experience testifies, anyone can be a blogger or published author. Therefore, as Christ followers, we must be all the more diligent to know the truth and recognize error.

> "For the time will come when men will not put up with sound doctrine. Instead, to suit their own desires, they will gather around them a great number of teachers to say what their itching ears want to hear. They will turn their ears away from the truth and turn aside to myths" (2 Timothy 4:3-4).

For this reason, I take seminary classes in biblical studies and strive to learn and grow so that I may never lead someone into error. I pray daily that God would use me to share only truth. In the last few years, I have read many articles by progressive Christians that pervert the Scriptures in order to support their beliefs, mostly in what appears to be an attempt to be socially accepting and affirming of all lifestyles and opinions.

While as Christians, we should be loving and accepting towards all people, we still must stand on the truths of Scripture, not wavering on the essential truths of the faith.

Damaris was a woman who lived in a time much the same as ours. She was a citizen of Athens in the first century, when philosophies and intellectual ideas abounded, not only in the university but also in the marketplace.

Several centuries earlier, the Greek Empire had excelled in art, literature, and philosophy. Socrates, Plato, and Aristotle led the way in philosophy and higher education. By the time Paul landed in Athens, the city was full of idols as well as those who debated different philosophies about life.

Stoics believed in living with nature and avoiding emotional experiences and desires. Epicureans taught that life was all about pleasure and seeking one's own happiness. When Paul arrived in Athens, he "reasoned with the Jews and the God-fearing Greeks, as well as in the marketplace day by day with those who happened to be there" (Acts 17:17).

According to Luke, the writer of Acts, the people became very interested in what Paul was sharing.

> "(All the Athenians and the foreigners who lived there spent their time doing nothing but talking about and listening to the latest ideas)" (Acts 17:21).

Sound familiar? Sometimes I feel that's all our society does anymore. We fall prey to fake news and become embroiled in controversies because our itching ears want to be convinced that

191

our way of living is okay. If we talk about it long enough or follow the right influencer, we can convince ourselves that we're okay, you're okay, and we're all okay.

But the truth is that we are all sinners, and apart from the mercy of God shown through His Son Jesus, we are all deserving of death (Romans 3:23, 6:23). Without Jesus, we are not okay. In a culture of confusion and chaos about God, knowledge, and life, Paul shared truth.

> "'The God who made the world and everything in it is the Lord of heaven and earth and does not live in temples built by hands. And he is not served by human hands, as if he needed anything, because he himself gives all men life and breath and everything else'" (Acts 17:24-25).

Paul established God as Creator, which conflicted with the views of many Greeks, who feared offending any god, and the Stoics, who believed God was part of nature.

> "'From one man he made every nation of men, that they should inhabit the whole earth; he determined the times set for them and the exact places where they should live'" (Acts 17:26).

Paul taught that God is sovereign over every aspect of life, which conflicted with the ideas of the Epicureans, who believed things were left to chance.

> "'God did this so that men would seek him and perhaps reach out for him and find him, though he is not far from each one of us. "For in him we live and move and have our being." As

some of your own poets have said, "We are his offspring"'"
(Acts 17:27-28).

Paul then quoted two of the Greeks' own poets. He used their own
ideas to lead them to truth.

> "'Therefore since we are God's offspring, we should not think
> that the divine being is like gold or silver or stone—an image
> made by man's design and skill. In the past God overlooked
> such ignorance, but now he commands all people everywhere
> to repent. For he has set a day when he will judge the world
> with justice by the man he has appointed. He has given proof
> of this to all men by raising him from the dead'" (Acts 17:29-
> 30).

Paul then presented them with the Gospel of repentance and
salvation through Jesus Christ, who was crucified, buried, and
raised from the dead.

> "When they heard about the resurrection of the dead, some of
> them sneered, but others said, 'We want to hear you again on
> this subject.' At that, Paul left the Council. A few men became
> followers of Paul and believed. Among them was Dionysius, a
> member of the Areopagus, also a woman named Damaris, and
> a number of others" (Acts 17:32-34).

Just as we can sometimes become confused about what is true in
our culture, I'm sure Damaris had similar questions. Because she
was present at the meeting of the Areopagus, many believe she was
a woman of means and intelligence.

She probably had listened to many debates among scholars and thinkers of the day, often with very differing views. We sometimes can hear two sides of an issue, and both sides seem compelling. How do we know what is true?

Many will tell us that truth is relative. They believe there is no standard of truth because no one can really know what is true. But if we say that we can't know truth, our very statement can't be true.

And if we say what is true for you is your truth, and what is true for me is my truth, we are saying two possibly opposite ideas can both be true. But two opposite ideas cannot both be true at the same time and in the same sense.

Truth is what matches reality. And it is not subject to the individual; truth is absolute.

> "This is the disciple who testifies to these things and who wrote them down. We know that his testimony is true" (John 21:24).

John's testimony corresponded to reality, because there were others who witnessed to this truth. If we want to know truth, we need to read and study the Word of God, the source of all truth.

We can easily be deceived by the many ideas and philosophies we hear today, even as Christians. If our theology is derived from memes and blog posts, rather than Scripture, we need to turn back to the Word.

> "See to it that no one takes you captive through hollow and deceptive philosophy, which depends on human tradition and

the basic principles of this world rather than on Christ" (Colossians 2:8).

Damaris responded to the truth when she heard it. May we be so rooted and grounded in the Word of God, that we too can respond to truth and reject what does not line up. Only then can we obey the Great Commission to make disciples, teaching them to obey what Christ has commanded (Matthew 29:19-20).

THE SEARCH FOR COURAGE

∽

IN A WORLD OF FEAR

MAKING TOUGH DECISIONS: RAHAB

———— ⟨∽⟩ ————

A very wise woman once counseled me to turn down a volunteer position at church because it would take time away from my family, especially my daughter who was in high school at the time. Mind you, she wasn't saying that church service wasn't important. I was already busy and serving in my church, teaching full-time, and involved in many after-school activities.

Her point was that I had only a few years left with Bethany at home, and that I should make the most of that time, since our role as disciple makers should begin with our own children. God first, family second, then church and other ministries.

I didn't listen. I wanted to appear spiritual and busy and important, so I agreed to the position. Looking back, I missed out on a lot of conversations and connections with my daughter because I was always busy.

Often in life we are faced with decisions that on the surface may seem simple or insignificant, but could in fact be life-changing for us or someone else.

Rahab was a woman faced with a momentous decision: Obey the king and probably be financially rewarded or hide two Jewish spies and probably be killed. From our view, we probably see it as a no-brainer because we know the story.

But Rahab didn't.

> "Then Joshua son of Nun secretly sent two spies from Shittim. 'Go, look over the land,' he said, 'especially Jericho.' So they went and entered the house of a prostitute named Rahab and stayed there" (Joshua 2:1).

The Jewish historian Jospehus and some other early sources identify Rahab as an innkeeper. The Hebrew word here indicates *prostitute*, as do the Greek in both Hebrews and James, so more than likely, she was both.

> "The king of Jericho was told, 'Look! Some of the Israelites have come here to spy out the land.' So the king of Jericho sent this message to Rahab: 'Bring out the men who came to you and entered your house, because they have come to spy out the whole land'" (Joshua 2:2-3).

Rahab was faced with a great decision. She could be obedient to the king and maybe make a little extra coin, or she could hide the enemy spies and risk losing her business and her life. How did this Canaanite woman make the decision to protect these two Israelite spies?

She made the decision in faith.

> "Before the spies lay down for the night, she went up on the roof and said to them, 'I know that the LORD has given this land to you and that a great fear of you has fallen on us, so that all who live in this country are melting in fear because of

you. We have heard how the LORD dried up the water of the Red Sea for you when you came out of Egypt, and what you did to Sihon and Og, the two kings of the Amorites east of the Jordan, whom you completely destroyed. When we heard of it, our hearts melted and everyone's courage failed because of you, for the LORD your God is God in heaven above and on the earth below'" (Joshua 2:8-11).

Rahab confessed here that she believed in the God of the Israelites. She had heard the truth of what God had done for them, and in healthy fear of God, she believed. The God of Israel was more powerful than the so-called gods of her people, and she was ready to receive that truth. God sent those Israelite spies to Rahab because He knew her heart. She was open to the truth and ready to act on it.

> "By faith the prostitute Rahab, because she welcomed the spies, was not killed with those who were disobedient" (Hebrews 11:31).

Rahab acted in response to her faith in the God of the Israelites. She may not yet have understood the covenant or the law, but she understood enough to respond in faith. We don't have to understand everything to follow God. Sometimes the things He calls us to do don't make sense to our human understanding or our flesh. But He will grow us as we commit ourselves to follow His leading.

Rahab's faith was demonstrated by her action.

James said that faith without action is dead (James 2:17). We express our faith in God when we follow Him in obedience even when we don't understand or even when the cost is high.

> "In the same way, was not even Rahab the prostitute considered righteous for what she did when she gave lodging to the spies and sent them off in a different direction? As the body without the spirit is dead, so faith without deeds is dead" (James 2:25-26).

Genuine faith will be demonstrated in action. But it will also be rewarded.

> "But Joshua spared Rahab the prostitute, with her family and all who belonged to her, because she hid the men Joshua had sent as spies to Jericho—and she lives among the Israelites to this day" (Joshua 2:25).

Rahab and her family—Gentiles—were given a place among the Israelites because she believed in their God by faith, and she acted on that belief. As followers of Christ, we are given a place among the redeemed because we believe in Jesus by faith, and we act on that belief by choosing to turn from our sins and follow Him.

> "A record of the genealogy of Jesus Christ the son of David, the son of Abraham: Abraham was the father of Isaac, Isaac the father of Jacob, Jacob the father of Judah and his brothers...Salmon the father of Boaz whose mother was Rahab..." (Matthew 1:1-2, 5a).

And, like Rahab, we too will find our place in Christ's genealogy as we become co-heirs with Christ and forever children of the King.

Maybe you haven't quite been ready to receive and act on the truth that Jesus is Lord. You don't have to understand everything or get your life together first. All you have to do is believe by faith that you (like all of us) are a sinner and that Jesus is the Son of God who died to pay the price for your sin.

Accept by faith what Christ has done for you on the cross. Make a decision to follow Jesus and trust that He will teach you what you need to know. Then get into His Word and find a good church to help you grow.

(Go to the end of this book to find out how to have new life in Jesus.)

Maybe you are a Christ-follower who is faced with a decision that seems right on the surface, but something is telling you to go the other way. It may mean the loss of money, prestige, or power, but like Rahab, you feel compelled to follow God's leading.

When it comes to making tough decisions, seek the Lord through prayer and His Word, seek the counsel of a mature Christian whom you trust, and then act on your faith in the one true God.

God may be calling us out of our comfort zone to do something scary. He may be calling us to give up something "spiritual" or something lucrative so we can focus on being present in our homes. Or He may be just calling us to Himself. Whatever the call, let's respond as Rahab did with both faith and action. He is a rewarder of those who seek Him.

"And without faith it is impossible to please God, because anyone who comes to him must believe that he exists and that he rewards those who earnestly seek him" (Hebrews 11:9).

Trust God to give you the courage to step out.

WISDOM IN RELATIONSHIPS: ABIGAIL

―――――――― ⌀ ――――――――

I tossed and turned, kicking off the covers, snuggling back beneath them, desperately trying to find some spot of comfort so I could rest. Truth be told, it wasn't my body that was struggling for relief—it was my mind. I was dealing with a relationship in which someone I loved was in the wrong in a big way. I knew it needed to be addressed, but I didn't want to be the one to do it.

Finally, I was so miserable, I told the Lord I would do whatever He asked of me. I sought His wisdom, and He gave me the Scripture and the words He wanted me to share.

> "If any of you lacks wisdom, he should ask God, who gives generously to all without finding fault, and it will be given to him" (James 1:5).

Have you ever been in a situation in which you knew you needed to confront something, but you were so perplexed by indecision and doubt that you couldn't find rest for your soul?

Abigail comes to mind as a woman of great wisdom. When faced with a foolish husband on one hand and an army coming against them on the other, Abigail had to make a life and death decision.

Abigail was married to Nabal, a very wealthy but mean and foolish man. David and his men, on the run from Saul, were nearby and needed food. Because David's men had protected Nabal's shepherds and treated them well, David expected that Nabal would return the favor with provisions (1 Samuel 25:1-8).

But Nabal was not a nice man, so he refused. When David got word, he told his men to arm up. He and 400 men set out to attack Nabal, intending to kill him and all his men (12-13). One of Nabal's servants warned Abigail.

> "'David sent messengers from the desert to give our master his greetings, but he hurled insults at them. Yet these men were very good to us. They did not mistreat us, and the whole time we were out in the fields near them nothing was missing. Night and day they were a wall around us all the time we were herding our sheep near them'" (1 Samuel 25:14b-16).

The servant knew that what his master did was wrong, so he appealed to the wisdom of his master's wife. All their lives were at stake.

> "'Now think it over and see what you can do, because disaster is hanging over our master and his whole household. He is such a wicked man that no one can talk to him'" (1 Samuel 25:17).

Abigail wasted no time coming up with a plan. She had the servants prepare food for David and his men and went out to meet him. Abigail knew that her husband's foolish behavior put all of them in jeopardy. Had she done nothing, David would have shed innocent blood.

"My brothers, if one of you should wander from the truth and someone should bring him back, remember this: Whoever turns a sinner from the error of his way will save him from death and cover over a multitude of sins" (James 5:19-20).

Sometimes God is calling us to be the one to confront a situation. It's never easy, but He will give us the wisdom and courage we need to do so.

"When Abigail saw David, she quickly got off her donkey and bowed down before David with her face to the ground" (1 Samuel 25:23).

Abigail came before David in a spirit of humility and gentleness. She brought with her the provisions his men needed. She mediated the situation and asked David to overlook her husband's foolishness and instead accept her apology on his behalf.

If God calls us to confront an issue, we should always approach the situation with humility and gentleness. If our desire is to be vindicated or to seek to be "right" rather than a desire to help the other person grow in her relationship with the Lord, then we are out of the will of God.

"Brothers, if someone is caught in a sin, you who are spiritual should restore him gently. But watch yourself, or you also may be tempted" (Galatians 6:1).

The temptation is to think more highly of ourselves than we ought. We need to seek the Lord and a spirit of humility first.

Abigail was careful to not blame David, but she pointed out to him the importance of serving God and not shedding innocent blood.

"'When the LORD has done for my master every good thing he promised concerning him and has appointed him leader over Israel, my master will not have on his conscience the staggering burden of needless bloodshed or of having avenged himself'" (1 Samuel 25:30-31).

When we deal with a situation in a relationship, we should ask God to give us the words to say. He can prepare us in advance with Scripture as He did with me, or He may tell us to go and let His Spirit guide our words. Either way, we need to give careful thought to our words and seek to build up and not tear down.

"Then we will no longer be infants, tossed back and forth by the waves, and blown here and there by every wind of teaching and by the cunning and craftiness of men in their deceitful scheming. Instead, speaking the truth in love, we will in all things grow up into him who is the Head, that is, Christ" (Ephesians 4:14-15).

Paul is referring to spiritual maturity in this context. In other words, we have to be spiritually mature and know the Word before we seek to share it with others. We need to speak truth; but we have to do it in love and from a heart of love.

"David said to Abigail, 'Praise be to the LORD, the God of Israel, who has sent you today to meet me. May you be blessed for your good judgment and for keeping me from bloodshed this day and from avenging myself with my own hands'" (1 Samuel 25:32-33).

When we seek God's wisdom in dealing with our relationships, He will guide us to take action with humility and careful thought to our words, so that others may be blessed.

The story didn't end so well for Nabal. He died the next day. But things turned around for Abigail.

The Bible tells us that she was both beautiful and intelligent. Her marriage to Nabal could very well have been an arranged marriage that she had no hope of escaping. He was both mean and foolish, so she likely had been mistreated, but Abigail was a woman of honor who interceded on his behalf. Because she chose to walk in wisdom, God blessed her and brought her into a relationship with David, the future king.

Is there a situation you need to confront in a relationship? Don't hesitate to trust God with your difficulty, even if it means you have to confront with truth. Trust God to lead you with His wisdom as you seek Him.

Who knows? Your intervention could save someone from a lifetime of pain.

WOMEN WHO SPEAK TRUTH: DEBORAH

Do you have some women in your life who speak truth to you? You know, the kind that might get on your nerves sometimes, but you can count on them to tell you what you *need* to hear and not just what you *want* to hear.

As women of the Word, God calls us to not only surround ourselves with women who speak truth; He calls us to be that woman as well.

Deborah is a great example of a woman who spoke truth. As a prophetess and a judge, she not only spoke for God, but she judged matters between individuals. I'm sure she had to sometimes speak hard truth.

> "Deborah, a prophetess, the wife of Lappidoth, was leading Israel at that time. She held court under the Palm of Deborah between Ramah and Bethel in the hill country of Ephraim, and the Israelites came to her to have their disputes settled" (Judges 4:4-5).

During the time of the judges, Israel was in a cycle of disobedience, suffering, crying out for deliverance, and restoration through the leadership of a divinely-appointed deliverer.

God's anointing would come upon these judges as they would settle disputes and often lead in victory against their enemies. The Holy Spirit did not dwell in believers at that time, so the people would listen to the Word of the Lord spoken through these prophets.

We may not all be judges or prophets, but we all have probably had to settle a dispute or counsel a friend who is going astray. God might call us to share hard truth that we fear won't be well-received. In Deborah we see an example of how to be a woman who is brave enough to speak God's truth.

First, Deborah spoke the Word of the Lord.

> "She sent for Barak son of Abinoam from Kedesh in Naphtali and said to him, 'The LORD, the God of Israel commands you: "Go, take with you ten thousand men of Naphtali and Zebulun and lead the way to Mount Tabor. I will lure Sisera, the commander of Jabin's army with his chariots and his troops to the Kishon River and give him into your hands"' (Judges 4:6-7).

Deborah could not have shared this word from the Lord with Barak unless she had spent time with God and listened to His voice. As women of the Word, we have to be *in* the Word. We can't share what we don't know. We can't guide our children, counsel our friends, or share the gospel unless we are seeking God and listening for His voice.

But Deborah also had to share hard truth with Barak.

> "Barak said to her, 'If you go with me, I will go; but if you don't go with me, I won't go.'
>
> 'Very well,' Deborah said, 'I will go with you. But because of the way you are going about this, the honor will not be yours, for the LORD will hand Sisera over to a woman'" (Judges 4:8-9).

I'm sure those weren't the words Barak wanted to hear, but Deborah was brave enough to speak the words God wanted him to hear. We definitely shouldn't try to counsel someone without the leadership of the Holy Spirit and His Word.

> "We have not received the spirit of the world but the Spirit who is from God, that we may understand what God has freely given us. This is what we speak, not in words taught us by human wisdom but in words taught by the Spirit, expressing spiritual truths in spiritual words" (1 Corinthians 2:12-13).

We must seek God and His truth, be led by His Spirit, and not speak what we think someone wants to hear or what will garner more praise for ourselves. We must speak truth.

Second, she spoke words of encouragement.

When Barak was hesitant to go into battle against 900 iron chariots, Deborah encouraged him, not with flattery about what *he* could do, but with encouragement about what God had already done.

"Then Deborah said to Barak, 'Go! This is the day the LORD has given Sisera into your hands. Has not the LORD gone ahead of you?'" (Judges 4:14).

God calls us to speak words of encouragement that build others up—not with false hope but with real truth. Again, in order to do so, we have to be spending time in the Word.

"The Sovereign LORD has given me an instructed tongue, to know the word that sustains the weary. He wakens me morning by morning, wakens my ear to listen like one being taught" (Isaiah 50:4).

Within our circle of friends, we all have those who need a word of encouragement. As we are led by the Spirit, He will give us words that can comfort, strengthen, and build up those around us.

"Therefore encourage one another and build each other up, just as in fact you are doing" (1 Thessalonians 5:11).

Third, Deborah spoke words of praise to God.

"'Hear this, you kings! Listen, you rulers! I will sing to the LORD, I will sing; I will make music to the LORD, the God of Israel'" (Judges 5:3).

Deborah realized the truth: victory didn't come as a result of their own efforts; the victory belonged to the Lord. Rather than taking credit for the win, she sang words of praise to God.

"If anyone speaks, he should do it as one speaking the very words of God. If anyone serves, he should do it with the strength God provides, so that in all things God may be praised through Jesus Christ. To him be the glory and the power forever and ever. Amen" (1 Peter 4:11).

As women who speak truth, we must seek God and listen for His voice, willing to speak truth to others, even when it may be hard to hear. When our friends are experiencing trials, our platitudes won't suffice. They need truth.

We need to share words of encouragement in the Lord, not just empty flattery that makes others feel good but may not be honest. Flattery is really pride—just a way of getting people to like us.

And we need to give God the glory for all He has done rather than taking credit for ourselves. Praise Him and sing to Him. Show the world that you give God the glory for what He has done.

If we do this, we will be women who speak truth. And even if that truth isn't immediately welcomed, we can rest in the assurance that if God is in it, He will use it for good and for His glory.

> "As the rain and the snow come down from heaven, and do not return to it without watering the earth and making it bud and flourish, so that it yields seed for the sower and bread for the eater, so is my word that goes out from my mouth: It will not return to me empty, but will accomplish what I desire and achieve the purpose for which I sent it" (Isaiah 55:10-11).

AT THE CROSSROADS OF COMFORT AND UNCERTAINTY: RUTH

———— ⟨∞⟩ ————

It's scary to leave behind what you know and step out into something new God may be calling you to. I spent twenty-two years in Christian education. It's what I was trained to do. It's what I love to do. It's what I know.

When God called me out of the classroom, I had to leave behind the comfort of the familiar for the uncertainty of the unknown. There was some excitement, of course, but the fear and anxiety of stepping out into something foreign still keep me awake some nights.

Have you ever been at that crossroads of decision, where you had to make a choice between something comfortable and familiar and a new venture that seemed scary and uncertain? Perhaps you are there now.

Another woman once stood at that junction. Ruth was a Moabite woman married to a Hebrew man whose family had fled Judah during a famine. The Moabites worshiped pagan gods, but Ruth was introduced through her husband's family to the God of the Jews—the One True God.

When her husband died, as well as his brother and father, Ruth's mother-in-law, Naomi, decided to return to Bethlehem, where she heard the famine was over. She and her two daughters-in-law "set out on the road that would take them back to the land of Judah" (Ruth 1:7b).

But then they came to a crossroads. Naomi thought about the future prospects of these two women. She had grown to love them, and they were all she had left of her family. Yet she realized that as Moabite women they stood little chance of future marriage in Judah.

It wasn't against the Law for an Israelite to marry a Moabite, but no Moabite could "enter the assembly of the LORD" (Deuteronomy 23:3). I'm sure Naomi was thinking that no one would marry them, and as widows with no male heirs, they would all be doomed to a life of poverty.

So, Naomi urged the girls to go back to their home, where they would at least have their own families, security, and the prospect of future marriage—a more comfortable life. Ruth, however, would not go back.

> "But Ruth replied, 'Don't urge me to leave you or turn back from you. Where you go I will go, and where you stay I will stay. Your people will be my people and your God my God'" (Ruth 1:16).

I so love this account of Ruth's devotion, because she clearly was intent not only to follow Naomi into a foreign land, but to follow the God of her husband and his family. Choosing to follow the call of God into the unknown is risky and uncertain. We may fear financial loss, rejection, and failure. The choice to follow God may even seem unreasonable to others.

For Ruth, a Moabitess, to live in Judah among the Israelites probably seemed ridiculous to her own family. But Ruth was following the call of God on her life. As my friend Michelle says, "She ended up with barley, Boaz, and a baby!" You see, because of Ruth's faithfulness to Naomi and Naomi's God, she was rewarded with blessings at every turn.

When they arrived in Judah, she went out to glean the barley fields so that she and Naomi would have food to eat. God was faithful to lead her to the right field. This story comes during the time of the Judges, a period of moral decline when everyone did what was right in his own eyes. To end up at the wrong field could have been dangerous.

But God sent Ruth to the fields of a man named Boaz, who was kind and generous and followed the Law which commanded farmers to leave behind some of their harvest for the poor to glean (Leviticus 19:9-10). Not only that, but he made provision for her to glean in abundance (Ruth 2:15-16).

In God's providence, Boaz was related to Naomi's husband, which meant that as a kinsman redeemer, he had the opportunity to marry Ruth, thereby redeeming the land and providing security, protection, and an heir to carry on the name (Deuteronomy 25:5-10, Leviticus 25:25-28).

Out of Ruth's marriage to Boaz came a baby. The devastation of loss in their family was redeemed through an heir, not just to keep the family line intact, but also to be the one through whom the Messiah would eventually come (Matthew 1:5).

Barley, Boaz, and a baby—the provision, protection, and promise of God—all the result of Ruth's faith and devotion.

What about us? When faced with the uncertain and uncomfortable call of God on our lives, will we choose the right path that leads to God's blessings? Will we trust Him for provision, protection, and promise?

The path may be difficult, fearful, and not without risk; but the blessings of obedience far exceed the consequences of not following God. And the good news is that as long as we stay with God, He will take care of us.

> "The Lord himself goes before you and will be with you; he will never leave you nor forsake you. Do not be afraid; do not be discouraged." (Deuteronomy 31:8).

These words spoken to Joshua still hold true for us today. So, what are you waiting for? Go ahead and choose that path you know God is calling you to, even if the thought makes you break out in a cold sweat. And if you're standing at the crossroads unsure which way to go, fast, pray, and give it to God. He knows your heart, and if you are willing to obey whatever He calls you to do, He will show you the way to go.

"Yet not as I will, but as you will" (Matthew 26:39b).

Through prayer, obedience, and faith, you will know if you are headed in the wrong direction, and God will honor your faithfulness and get you back on track. Following God is not for the faint-hearted; but nothing compares with the peace, joy, and adventure of being on mission with the King!

PREPARED
TO SHARE TRUTH:
HULDAH

About a year ago, I was at a coffee shop being interviewed about one of my books. After the discussion, I sat down and struck up a conversation with a young man. He had heard the interview, and as we talked, he shared that he was an atheist.

I really enjoyed my conversation with him. He was intelligent, listened to my responses, and countered with some ideas of his own. I was ready to talk ('cause I'm a talker and I love getting to know new people), but not as prepared to share truth with him as I wish I had been.

Huldah was recognized as one who heard from the Lord. When the king of Judah needed guidance from God, she was sought out for the answers.

You see, Josiah became king at the age of eight. His father had not followed the ways of God, and the people no longer sought the God of Israel. They had erected altars to false gods, leaving the temple of God in disrepair.

By the age of sixteen, Josiah had begun to seek the Lord. In just a few years, he had the evil altars torn down and their idols destroyed. Over the next few years, the king had the temple repaired and restored as well. While working on those repairs, the high priest found something that changed everything.

> "While they were bringing out the money that had been taken into the temple of the LORD, Hilkiah the priest found the Book of the Law of the LORD that had been given through Moses" (2 Chronicles 34:14).

When the words of the Law were read to Josiah, he realized that his people had been living in rebellion to the God they claimed to worship.

> "When the king heard the words of the Law, he tore his robes" (2 Chronicles 34:19).

Tearing the robes was a sign of great sorrow and despair. Josiah's heart was broken when he heard the truth of God's Word. He asked for the high priest to "go and inquire of the LORD" for him and the people, because he knew God's anger must burn against them for their apostasy.

The high priest could have consulted the prophets of that day, Jeremiah or Zephaniah, but for some reason he sought out a woman named Huldah.

> "Hilkiah and those the king had sent with him went to speak to the prophetess Huldah, who was the wife of Shallum son of Tokhath, the son of Hasrah, keeper of the wardrobe" (2 Chronicles 34:22).

Huldah was the wife of the keeper of the wardrobe, so maybe she was consulted because she was closer and more accessible. For whatever reason, she obviously was known as a woman who heard from God. Do people know us as women who are close to God? Do others seek us out when they need wisdom and discernment from the Lord?

If we follow Jesus, people should see something different about us. They should know that we are close to God and can share truth from His Word when they have a need. Huldah was consulted, and she didn't hesitate to share the truth.

> "She said to them, 'This is what the LORD, the God of Israel, says: Tell the man who sent you to me, "This is what the LORD says: I am going to bring disaster on this place and its people—all the curses written in the book that has been read in the presence of the king of Judah. Because they have forsaken me and burned incense to other gods and provoked me to anger by all that their hands have made, my anger will be poured out on this place and will not be quenched"'" (2 Chronicles 34:23-25).

First, Huldah was ready with the answers they sought. She didn't hesitate to share the word of God because she was already in tune with the Lord. And she was a wardrobe assistant, not a biblical scholar.

When we spend time with God in His Word and in prayer, our hearts will be close to His. As a result, we should have a word ready to share with them.

> "A word aptly spoken is like apples of gold in settings of silver" (Proverbs 25:11).

Second, Huldah was quick to say, "This is what the LORD, the God of Israel, says." She didn't share her opinion or give her ideas about the situation. She just shared the Word of God with them.

> "A fool finds no pleasure in understanding but delights in airing his own opinions" (Proverbs 18:2).

Third, Huldah didn't hesitate to share a difficult truth. I know we may sometimes dread conversations about topics of controversy in our culture. We don't want to seem intolerant. But we need to remember that it's not our opinion that matters. We can share that "this is what the Lord says," because God is not intolerant. He is a God of love who has offered mercy and grace to "whosoever" would believe by faith and receive Him in their hearts (John 3:16).

> "Instead, speaking the truth in love, we will in all things grow up into him who is the Head, that is, Christ" (Ephesians 4:15).

And Huldah trusted the power of God's Word to bring the change.

> "So they took her answer back to the king. Then the king called together all the elders of Judah and Jerusalem. He went up to the temple of the LORD with the men of Judah, the people of Jerusalem, the priests and the Levites—all the people from the least to the greatest. He read in their hearing all the words of the Book of the Covenant, which had been found in the temple of the LORD. The king stood by his pillar and renewed the covenant in the presence of the LORD—to follow the LORD and keep his commands, regulations, and decrees with all his heart and all his soul, and to obey the words of the covenant written in this book" (2 Chronicles 34:29-31).

God's Word has the power to change our lives, our families, our churches, and our nation. We don't have to have a seminary degree. We don't have to give our own opinion.

> "For the word of God is living and active. Sharper than any double-edged sword, it penetrates even to dividing soul and spirit, joints and marrow; it judges the thoughts and attitudes of the heart" (Hebrews 4:12).

But we should always be prepared to give the reason for the hope that we have.

> "But in your hearts set apart Christ as Lord. Always be prepared to give an answer to everyone who asks you to give the reason for the hope that you have. But do this with gentleness and respect, keeping a clear conscience, so that those who speak maliciously against your good behavior in Christ may be ashamed of their slander" (1 Peter 3:15-16).

If we want to be prepared to share God's truth when people need it, we must spend time with God, study His Word, pray for courage, and then trust the power of His Word to do what only He can do.

WOMEN WHO WELCOME: LYDIA

———— ⌒⌒ ————

When Kenneth and I were building our house, we were in awe of a God that would provide for us to do so. I have always been in Christian education, which is a financial sacrifice. So when God made a way for us to build on our family land, we promised our home would always be open for kingdom purposes.

But to be honest, hospitality is not really my gift. I love to be around people, but I'm not a super hostess. I tend to get caught up in conversation and forget to invite people to sit or ask if they would like a drink.

I cook because we like to eat, but I am no Betty Crocker. So I have shied away from having people over for dinner—especially when all the women I know can cook those down-home Southern country meals.

One of the women in the Bible who has always intrigued me, though, is Lydia. We only get four verses to figure out who she was, but to me she is a fantastic example of hospitality. Paul and his companions were on their second missionary journey when God led them to the city of Philippi, a Roman colony in eastern

Macedonia. Very few Jews lived there, so there was no synagogue. Luke described their arrival.

> "On the Sabbath we went outside the city gate to the river, where we expected to find a place of prayer. We sat down and began to speak to the women who had gathered there. One of those listening was a woman named Lydia, a dealer in purple cloth from the city of Thyatira, who was a worshiper of God. The Lord opened her heart to respond to Paul's message" (Acts 16:13-14).

Lydia was a Gentile businesswoman who had come to believe in the God of the Jews. She had already found a group of faithful women with whom she could join for prayer. Her heart was open to the message of the gospel. When she believed, she shared that message with her household, and all of them were saved and baptized. Her first act of service was to open her home to these missionaries.

> "When she and the members of her household were baptized, she invited us to her home. 'If you consider me a believer in the Lord,' she said, 'come and stay at my house.' And she persuaded us" (Acts 16:15).

I love this story! Lydia was eager for community and fellowship with other believers. She wanted to open not just her heart but also her home to God. Lydia persuaded these missionaries that she wanted them to stay.

I don't know if Lydia had the "gift of hospitality" or not. Who knows whether or not she was a great cook or her home was perfectly decorated or everything was in its place. She just wanted to be around other believers. Her prerequisite was not a perfect home but her belief.

As I think about hospitality and what it means, three things stand out to me that I believe will help us grow in hospitality.

We welcome.

Once when Paul and the missionaries had been shipwrecked on an island, they were shown hospitality by the native chief official.

> "He welcomed us to his home and for three days entertained us hospitably" (Acts 28:7b).

The word translated *welcome* means "to receive or embrace."[13] This official showed kindness to the missionaries. He received them warmly and took care of them while on his island. I don't know exactly how he "entertained" them—maybe with conversation and a cup of hot tea. But the emphasis on this passage to me is the welcome—the warmness and kindness with which he received them.

Paul and his companions prayed for the official's father and healed him. Because this official was willing to receive the missionaries, he was blessed in return.

We honor.

Another characteristic of hospitality is honor. When we invite people into our home, we are showing them that we honor our relationship enough to make space for them in our lives.

"Love must be sincere. Hate what is evil; cling to what is good. Be devoted to one another in brotherly love. Honor one another above yourselves. Never be lacking in zeal, but keep your spiritual fervor, serving the Lord. Be joyful in hope, patient in affliction, faithful in prayer. Share with God's people who are in need. Practice hospitality" (Romans 12:9-13).

When we sincerely love others, we honor them. That honor can be shown by sharing our sofa, our coffee, our bread, or our prayers with one another. In a digital age in which we are so connected through our phones, we often fail to connect in person. We honor one another when we open our homes and invite others in. We show them that they are worth our time, our attention, and our real connection.

We serve.

I'll be honest; serving others does not come naturally to me. I have a friend whose primary gift is service. She is always ready with an open hand to give and to help others. Me—not so much. It's not that I don't want to serve; it's just not my first reaction to others. I want to talk and connect and pray. But guess what? Each of these gifts can be used to make others welcome.

"Offer hospitality to one another without grumbling. Each one should use whatever gift he has to serve others, faithfully administering God's grace in its various forms. If anyone speaks, he should do it as one speaking the very words of God. If anyone serves, he should do it with all the strength

God provides, so that in all things God may be praised through Jesus Christ" (1 Peter 4:9-11a).

The point is that our hearts and our attention should be on those we are inviting in. Whether or not I remember to offer them tea is not that important. But the fact that I want to embrace them, honor them, and connect with them is what reflects the love of Christ.

Jesus has called us to make disciples. Sometimes we will need to open the front door and invite someone to come sit at the table with us in order to build a relationship with her. Sometimes hospitality will look like a dining room table covered in Bibles, laughter, chips, and salsa.

At times, we may be able to welcome missionaries to our home for a furlough, or we may get to open a spare room to a foster child. God calls us to show hospitality for the sake of the gospel.

"We ought therefore to show hospitality to such people so that we may work together for the truth" (3 John 8).

We are all working together for the truth, so how can we open up our lives in a way that extends a welcome, shows honor, and serves those around us with Christ's love? We don't have to have a perfect home or be the perfect hostess. We don't need someone else's gift to be hospitable. We just need to love people like Jesus did.

We follow Jesus' example.

Because He has opened His arms to us and received us as His own; He has honored us enough to die for us; and He has served us through His example. Remember our girl Lydia who was so eager to invite the missionaries to stay? She ended up planting the first church in Philippi.

> "After Paul and Silas came out of the prison, they went to Lydia's house, where they met with the brothers and encouraged them" (Acts 16:40).

Maybe you have a neighbor God has put on your heart to have over for dinner. Perhaps the Holy Spirit has been nudging you to start a home Bible study. Or maybe you can host a missionary, exchange student, or foster child in your home.

God calls us to be hospitable, to open our hearts, our hands, and our homes to others that we might share with them His love and His truth. He will give us the courage to overcome our fear. Who needs your invitation today?

WOMEN WHO LEAD: LYDIA

Small group fellowships are a great opportunity for discipleship, accountability, and growing relationships. We often don't build those connections within the larger church community because of size, so the relationships I have developed within the context of a small group have been invaluable to my spiritual life.

Because Lydia opened her home to the disciples, she was in a unique position to learn and grow. I can't imagine the discussions that took place at her house with Paul, Timothy, Luke, and Silas under her roof! What a fantastic privilege to have been part of something so incredible!

But then I remember: she was just a woman who ran a business, who believed in God, and who was faithful to meet with others for prayer. She didn't know everything—but God saw her heart and used her. History tells us that a church grew out of her home.

The early church started as small groups that met in homes. Today, we have church bodies that meet collectively for worship and preaching of the Word. So why start a small group?

I can think of several reasons, but I love that it gives us the opportunity to make disciples as we grow and do life together.

"We loved you so much that we were delighted to share with you not only the gospel of God but our lives as well" (1 Thessalonians 2:8).

Paul reminded the Thessalonians in this passage that he had come to them in complete sincerity, willing to share his very life with them. I believe this is the heart of true discipleship.

We can invite people to church and to Sunday school (and should!), but small groups are more intimate, provide opportunities for people to ask questions, and allow for ministry to take place on a more personal level.

Jesus had thousands of followers, twelve apostles, but He also discipled one-on-one. I recommend finding one person with whom you can spend one-on-one time, as well. Just think, if each of us made it our goal to find one person to disciple, what a difference we could make in our communities!

I challenge you to find that one person and invite her to your small group; then suggest meeting together once a week—just the two of you.

Here are my five best tips for starting your own small group.

First, pray. Pray specifically for God to speak to you and show you if this is something He is calling you to do. Pray that He would lead you in every aspect of starting your small group.

Second, ask God to show you whom to invite. Decide on how you will invite them—in person, by email, paper invitation, Facebook group, etc. I recommend keeping your group small (8-12 people).

Third, choose a format for your study. Do you want to have refreshments or a meal? Adding a short time to share food together usually opens your group up and allows time to get to know each other. How long do you plan for your meeting to last? Let people know what to expect.

Fourth, choose a time and location. Work around your church's schedule. Talk with your pastor if you wish to meet at church. I recommend meeting in a home, which encourages your ladies to relax and share with each other. Discipleship is about doing real life together. Time spent together in your home will allow you to be vulnerable with the ladies you bring together.

Last, choose a Bible study carefully. Do you want a video-driven study, one with a small amount of homework, or a study that goes deep into the Word? This consideration will depend upon the ladies you invite. Unchurched ladies or new Christians may be more encouraged by lessons that are shorter; while others may desire to go deeper in God's Word.

If you are looking for a Bible study for your small group, I invite you to *consider Let's Run! Running the Race with Faith and Perseverance or Inside Out: How Intimacy with Jesus Changes Everything.*

Let's Run! is great for believers who are serving God but want to go deeper and learn more about what it means to walk by faith. *Inside Out* is a super option for unchurched ladies, new believers, or those who are familiar with church but don't understand what it means to have a personal relationship with Jesus.

Each week of both Bible studies ends with a Weekend Devo to summarize the lessons and give opportunity for thoughtful reflection and application. You can also find small group ideas at the end of each week.

If God has put that desire in your heart, then what are you waiting for? Start praying for the women He has put on your heart, and be ready to step out and make disciples. That's doing kingdom work!

SERVING THE LORD: PHOEBE

───────── ⟨∽⟩ ─────────

You have a call on your life.

If you love Jesus and have decided to follow Him, then He has equipped you with both spiritual gifts and natural talents that are to be used to further the gospel and build the kingdom. You are called to make disciples (Matthew 28:19), to teach (Matthew 28:20), and to preach the gospel (2 Timothy 4:2).

How you fulfill that calling can look differently for different women and in different seasons of life. For many years, I made little disciples in my home. As a teacher in Christian education, I also made disciples among my students. I have taught and made disciples in my church, both working with children and youth.

Now, God is calling me to share the gospel, to make disciples, and to encourage others in their spiritual growth through writing and teaching other women.

As women who want to serve Jesus well, we can sometimes struggle with our place, especially when controversy surrounds the issue. My desire is not to tell you what to believe but to give you the bigger picture of how Scripture informs our beliefs.

I have spent this past year studying and writing about women in the Bible because this topic was of interest to me. Let me encourage you to dig into the Word as well and to study these passages for yourself.

I love these 50 words Paul shares in his letter to the Romans, because they shed light on his support for women in ministry.

> "I commend to you our sister Phoebe, a servant of the church in Cenchrea. I ask you to receive her in a way worthy of the saints and to give her any help she may need from you, for she has been a great help to many people, including me" (Romans 16:1).

First, Paul calls her "our sister." Phoebe was a fellow believer and part of the family of God.

> "You are all sons of God through faith in Christ Jesus, for all of you who were baptized into Christ have clothed yourselves with Christ. There is neither Jew nor Greek, slave nor free, male nor female, for you are all one in Christ Jesus" (Galatians 3:26-28).

Second, Paul calls her "a servant of the church in Cenchrea." The word translated servant is *diakonos,* which means servant or minister. This role probably referred to her ministry to other women, possibly through baptizing, teaching, and caring for the needs of widows and orphans.

> "Jesus called them together and said, 'You know that the rulers of the Gentiles lord it over them, and their high officials exercise authority over them, Not so with you. Instead,

whoever wants to become great among you must be your servant" (Matthew 20:25-26).

Third, Paul calls her a helper, which from the original Greek, can be translated *benefactor* or *patron*. More than likely, Phoebe was a woman of financial means who helped support the spread of the gospel, as many women had supported Jesus.

> "After this, Jesus traveled about from one town and village to another, proclaiming the good news of the kingdom of God. The Twelve were with him, and also some women who had been cured of evil spirits and diseases: Mary (called Magdalene) from whom seven demons had come out; Joanna the wife of Cuza, the manager of Herod's household; Susanna; and many others. These women were helping to support them out of their own means" (Luke 8:1-3).

Just as Jesus had women disciples who followed Him and supported Him—unheard of in His culture—Paul also encouraged women in ministry.

Let's not forget, Phoebe was chosen to deliver the epistle to the Romans. Paul entrusted her with this important letter that spells out the gospel: how to be saved, the relationship between Jew and Gentile in God's plan of redemption, and what it means to walk in the righteousness of God.

Travel during those days was dangerous, and it was a good 700 miles by both sea and land to get from Cenchrea to Rome. We know from Paul's other letters that he sent them in the hands of people he knew and trusted. Phoebe fell into that category.

Dear sister in Christ, I understand the controversy that surrounds our role in ministry, but I believe we each need to get into the Word and pray and seek the Lord to guide us in how we fulfill the Great Commission.

Yes, there are some difficult passages in the New Testament in which Paul seems to be saying that women should be quiet in the church. We must be sure to study these passages and understand them in the proper context.

Paul also commended women for their service as fellow workers (Romans 16, Philippians 4:2-3). He assumed women were praying and prophesying in church (1 Corinthians 11:5).

And in fact, when he says women should learn in quietness and submission (1 Timothy 2:11) and ask their husband at home if they have questions (1 Corinthians 14:33-35), he is actually going beyond the cultural norms of that time to say that women should be learning the Word at all!

Both the Old and New Testaments are full of references to women who served God with the talents and gifts God gave them.

Sound interpretation involves considering the whole counsel of Scripture, not just a few passages that speak to an issue. And we have already covered how Jesus elevated women to a status that was definitely counter-cultural in His time.

Bottom line, it's our job to seek the Lord and His Word rather than just be informed by someone else's idea of what is right and wrong. Let's not get caught up in the emotionalism of the moment, but rather let's be committed to prayer and Bible study so that we can serve God well.

There are many ways to fulfill the Great Commission as women. How we do that is secondary to the reason for it, and that is the gospel message, which is desperately needed in our world today.

So, I hope that I have given you a desire to seek the Lord, to study His Word, and to serve Him with your whole heart in a way that brings Him glory. Let's allow God to use this struggle for His glory as we commit ourselves anew to serve Him well.

THE SEARCH FOR HOPE

IN A WORLD OF DESPAIR

WHEN YOU DON'T SEE GOD IN YOUR STORY: ESTHER

———————— ⌁ ————————

Life is hard. Disappointments, diagnoses, loss, and suffering are an inevitable part of our story. Sometimes we can really struggle to see where God fits into the narrative.

The account of Esther gives us a fantastic source of encouragement today. Critics have pondered for centuries why the book of Esther is even in the canon of Scripture—after all, God is never mentioned in her story.

Or is He?

True, we don't see His name, but we certainly see His hand. And that may be the most powerful lesson to come from this story about a beautiful girl who risked her life to save her people: When we live surrendered to God, He is at work even when we can't see Him.

This is the story of God from start to finish. In the life of this young Jewish girl, we see the sovereignty, support, and salvation of God. And then we don't hear from Esther in Scripture again. Her life pointed to the One whose story does continue.

A person who believes in luck and coincidence would be blown away by this narrative. How fortunate that so many things happen to line up just right for Esther and her people, who were on the edge of extinction because of their "intolerance" amidst a polytheistic people!

While living in exile in Persia, Esther *just happened* to be selected by the king to replace his wife who displeased him. Esther's uncle Mordecai *happened* to uncover a plot to assassinate the king which left him in the king's favor. The king *just so happened* to lie awake one night and read over the history logs detailing Mordecai's loyalty.

All of these events led to the moment in which Esther brought her request before the king. You see, in this pluralistic society, royal officials expected to be worshiped. Mordecai, a Jew who worshiped the one true God, refused. So Haman, the king's official, plotted to slaughter them all.

The Jewish people's only hope to avoid annihilation lay with a young Jewish girl who had the king's ear. Esther, whose Jewish heritage had been kept quiet, was now in a position to go before the king and ask for mercy.

"And who knows but that you have come to royal position for such a time as this?" (Esther 4:14b).

Esther just happened to be in the right place at the right time to intercede with the king on behalf of her people. Right? In truth, we know that the sovereignty of God led her to the palace. And there she was inspired to seek God's help and step out in faith.

Now to us, this may seem like a walk in the park. All she has to do as the new queen is go to the king and say "By the way, I'm a Jew. Please don't kill me and my family." But, alas, times were different. Anyone who approached the king without being invited would be executed unless he decided to extend his royal scepter and show mercy. Esther had to take that chance in order to intercede for her people.

To say this was a risk is an understatement. But Esther didn't go to the king alone. She called on the support of her God.

> "Then Esther sent this reply to Mordecai: 'Go, gather together all the Jews who are in Susa, and fast for me. Do no eat or drink for three days, night or day. I and my maids will fast as you do. When this is done, I will go to the king, even though it is against the law. And if I perish, I perish'" (Esther 4:15-16).

Esther risked her life to go before the king and ask for help. But she didn't go unprepared. Fasting was always accompanied by prayer. Esther called on the people to go before God in humility, seeking His favor and support.

The writer of Esther, I believe, leaves God's name out intentionally to heighten the fact that He is at work behind the scenes, even when we can't see Him. He is sovereign over circumstance and coincidence, and He is supporting us in our time of need.

Esther's adventure may seem void of God; it was anything but. In His sovereign power, the God of the Jews was working in the midst of their crisis. He orchestrated circumstances and events to bring about the deliverance of His people. Esther knew she was powerless to control her circumstances, but through fasting and prayer, she called on the support of the One who was not.

This beautiful account of the sovereignty and support of God concludes with the salvation of the Jewish people from extinction. The king's favor was extended to Esther, and through a series of "fortunate" events, the evil Haman was hanged and Mordecai was honored.

The Jews were allowed to defend themselves and won the victory. We may not see "G-o-d" in Esther's story, but He is there. And He's in your story, too. In fact, He's the Author of your chronicle. Even when you can't see Him, He's behind the scenes, working on your behalf, supporting you in your time of need, and making a way for you to know Him more.

> "Let us fix our eyes on Jesus, the author and perfecter of our faith, who for the joy set before him endured the cross, scorning its shame, and sat down at the right hand of the throne of God" (Hebrews 12:2).

We don't serve a God who leaves us in the midst of our suffering, nor One who promises we won't suffer. We serve a God who has also suffered, is with us in the midst of the pain, and will work in our lives for our good and His glory.

> "And we know that in all things God works for the good of those who love him, who have been called according to his purpose" (Romans 8:28).

Even when we can't see Him.

My friend, if you are in a time of suffering, disappointment, or pain, I pray you will look to the Author of your story. Out of our greatest pain we sometimes see Him best.

Like Esther, we too can surrender our lives into His care, trusting Him with the plot, the characters, and the outcome of our drama. When we do, our story becomes His story, and that's an adventure that never ends.

JESUS SHOWED COMPASSION TO WOMEN: THE WIDOW OF NAIN

———————— ∽ ————————

What pain or heartache do you find yourself in today? What struggles have gripped your heart with fear and anxiety?

I have a beautiful story to share with you today—not a new revelation or a fresh word from God you've never heard before. I want to share a timeless truth from an eternal Word that never grows old or becomes irrelevant.

I have been so moved by this short narrative of a widow who was burying her only son. You see, in her day, she had no opportunity for employment, insurance, or a 501-K. All her livelihood was tied up in those two men. And they were gone.

> "Soon afterward, Jesus went to a town called Nain, and his disciples and a large crowd went along with him. As he approached the town gate, a dead person was being carried out—the only son of his mother, and she was a widow. And a large crowd was with her" (Luke 7:11-12).

A large crowd with Him and a large crowd with her—can you picture all these people moving in opposite directions through the town gate? Jesus had been busy teaching, healing, and leading His disciples, but when He saw this woman, his heart was moved.

> "When the Lord saw her, his heart went out to her and he said, 'Don't cry'" (Luke 7:13).

Honestly, I can't even read that verse without a gigantic lump in my throat. The tenderness of our Savior! I can't imagine losing my husband. But many of you have. I don't want to think about losing a child. But some of you are there right now.

When I think of the pain, the loss, and the hopelessness she must have felt, I just want to curl up in a ball and cry for her. But God. God in human form met her at that gate, looked her in the eyes, and said, "Don't cry. I'm here now."

You know why? Because He is compassion. He is love. He sees our hearts; He hears our cries; He knows our pain. And His heart goes out.

> "Then he went up and touched the coffin, and those carrying it stood still. He said, 'Young man, I say to you, get up!' The dead man sat up and began to talk, and Jesus gave him back to his mother" (Luke 7:14-15).

Can you imagine what the young man began saying when he sat up and realized he was alive? Can you imagine his mama's joy? She got him back. Her loss was returned. Her pain was soothed. Her future was restored.

Jesus hates death. He hates the pain and suffering it causes. That's why He was willing to touch an unclean coffin. That's why He went to the cross and conquered death once for all. That's why He came back on the third day.

Jesus' victory over death is the hope that we all have. Sin in this world is what leads to death (Genesis 3), but Jesus offers us life.

> "This grace was given us in Christ Jesus before the beginning of time, but it has now been revealed through the appearing of our Savior, Jesus Christ, who has destroyed death and has brought life and immortality to light through the gospel" (2 Timothy 1:9b-10).

Jesus may not raise our loved ones here and now, but if they belong to Him, they will be raised to life, and we will spend eternity together. Even in our loss, Jesus can still look us in the eye and say, "Don't cry." Because He is here. He has conquered death, hell, and the grave. He is still moved with compassion in our losses.

And He is still able to give us back what we have lost. Our pain soothed by His touch. Our hope restored for the future.

For me, this story not only demonstrates the heart of God for us, but it also challenges me to share the gospel with those I care about. The hope of resurrection is for those who belong to Jesus. When I remember that we are mortal, and this world is not our home, I am even more motivated to share the love and truth of Jesus with those around me.

> "Since, then, you have been raised with Christ, set your hearts on things above, where Christ is seated at the right hand of God. Set your minds on things above, not on earthly things" (Colossians 3:1-2).

We don't hear from our widow and her son again after their encounter with Jesus, but you can bet their lives were never the same. When we encounter death, loss, pain, and struggles, we too can experience the tender touch of the Savior.

We too can allow His love and compassion in going to the cross to move us from death to life. We can hope again. We can smile again. Because Jesus is here.

JUST KEEP SHOWING UP: THE WOMAN WITH THE ISSUE OF BLOOD

──────────── ⟡ ────────────

This past weekend I was so blessed to be able to take a retreat with my Bible girlfriends to the mountains. We go once a year to Icthus Ministries in Bryson City, NC for a weekend of rest, worship, Bible study, fellowship, and fun together. (And did I mention good food?)

The couple who runs the retreat center, Bill and Edith Dingle, are two of the most loving, Spirit-filled people I know. When we arrived, Bill shared a story with me that I want to share with you because it was a great encouragement for our walk with the Lord.

Edith and their daughter Emma are cloggers. In fact, they are pretty good cloggers, winning the National Championship in Nashville, TN. That's right, they won a National Championship!

With the title came a huge trophy and all the bragging rights you can imagine. Not to mention, they have now been invited to the World Championship! What an amazing accomplishment (even though they had no competition)!

No, it's not that the competitors were bad cloggers. There was literally no competition. Nobody else showed up! So, even though

Edith and Emma worked really hard, put in untold hours of practice, and drove to Nashville for the competition, they won a championship because they showed up when no one else did.

How like our God to honor their faithfulness!

As Bill shared with me, sometimes the Lord will make us champions because we just keep showing up, even when it's a struggle, even when everything may seem to be against us, even when it costs us something.

I am reminded of the woman with the issue of blood.

> "A large crowd followed and pressed around him. And a woman was there who had been subject to bleeding for twelve years. She had suffered a great deal under the care of many doctors and had spent all she had, yet instead of getting better she grew worse" (Mark 5:24b-26).

Here's a woman who had every reason to not show up. Her medical problem, probably female in nature, made her ceremonially unclean (Leviticus 15:25-33). So she would have been shunned by others and unable to have contact with them. This sickness had ruled her life for twelve years, but she had not given up seeking help. She continued to seek doctors who could cure her, but they took her money while her condition only worsened.

By the time she heard the rumors about this man who could heal the sick, she could have just decided to stay home. What good would it do to show up for another disappointment? Another letdown? Another hopeless situation?

"When she heard about Jesus, she came up behind him in the crowd and touched his cloak, because she thought, 'If I just touch his clothes, I will be healed'" (Mark 5:27-28).

She did show up. And when the crowd was too large and pressing all around, she could have just retreated and gone back home. After all, what good would it do anyway?

But she didn't. She continued to press in and believe that all her hope would be rewarded with just a touch of His garment. And she was right.

> "Immediately her bleeding stopped and she felt in her body that she was freed from her suffering" (Mark 5:29).

She won! She took home the trophy—no more pain, no more suffering, no more enduring the rejection of others. Because she just kept showing up. She kept seeking and believing that one day she would be made whole again.

I know sometimes you're tired of doing church and ministry. You're weary of fighting spiritual battles. You've endured rejection or hoped for an answer to a particular prayer with no result. Sometimes it would be easier to just throw in the towel. But God says you are more than a conqueror in Him.

> "No, in all these things [trouble, hardship, persecution] we are more than conquerors through him who loved us" (Romans 8:37, brackets added from v.35).

Keep praying. Keep seeking. Keep striving to be what God wants you to be. He rewards those who diligently seek Him (Hebrews 11:6). No matter the cost, no matter the struggle, regardless of the effort—don't give up, my friend. Keep walking in obedience to what God has called you to do.

> "This is the victory that overcomes the world, even our faith" (1 John 5:4b).

So just keep showing up. At the end of the day, you are taking home the trophy. Because you are already a champion in Him.

WOMEN WHO STAYED AT THE CROSS

―――――――――― ⟨∞⟩ ――――――――――

Have you ever put all your hopes and dreams into something only to have it all fall apart? A death, divorce, diagnosis, or some other devastating circumstance can make us question all that we have known and trusted in.

For the women who followed Jesus, that dark day at Golgotha must have taken their breath away. These women had been saved, delivered, validated, and valued by Jesus. They trusted in Him, followed Him, sat as His feet and learned from Him. They had cared for His needs and supported His ministry out of their own resources. Yet on that fateful day, all must have seemed lost.

Helpless as they watched Jesus carry His own cross, confused as they witnessed Him mocked and beaten beyond recognition, heartbroken as He breathed His last on the cross—the women who followed Jesus must surely have despaired of life itself.

Yet, they stayed.

> "Many women were there, watching from a distance. They had followed Jesus from Galilee to care for his needs. Among them were Mary Magdalene, Mary the mother of James and Joses, and the mother of Zebedee's sons" (Matthew 27:55-56).

They were faithful to the very bitter end.

These women watched from a distance—hurt, broken, confused, but not turning back. At some point, a few of them drew near the cross, not wanting to remain apart from Him as He suffered.

> "Near the cross of Jesus stood his mother, his mother's sister, Mary the wife of Clopas, and Mary Magdalene" (John 19:25).

As Jesus was laid in a tomb, they stood watch over where His body lay.

> "Joseph took the body, wrapped it in a clean linen cloth, and placed it in his own new tomb that he had cut out of the rock. He rolled a big stone in front of the entrance to the tomb and went away. Mary Magdalene and the other Mary were sitting there opposite the tomb" (Matthew 27:59-61).

I can't imagine what was in their hearts and minds that day. Their devotion to the Messiah outweighed any fear they may have felt toward the Roman soldiers or religious leaders who demanded His death. Their love for Him overruled the despair, the questions, the doubt. Their gratitude was greater than their grief, and they couldn't leave His side.

Disappointed? Sure. Angry? Absolutely. Disillusioned? Maybe.

But walking away? Not on your life.

Jesus had loved them so deeply and completely, and they simply loved Him back. Even death couldn't quell their devotion.

Dear friend, I don't know what you have been through that might cause you to lose hope and give up on Jesus, but God wants you to know today that He loves you so deeply and completely that nothing can separate you from His love.

> "For I am convinced that neither death nor life, neither angels nor demons, neither the present nor the future, nor any powers, neither height nor depth, nor anything else in all creation, will be able to separate us from the love of God that is in Christ Jesus our Lord" (Romans 8:38-39).

Don't give up on God. Stay. Stay with Him even when it hurts. Remain in the Word even when you don't understand. Abide in His love even when it feels cold and distant.

Stay at the foot of the cross in worship. Wait by the tomb in prayer. It's not over yet. Jesus always gets the last word.

WOMEN WHO ARE MISTREATED

———————————— ᢉᡕᢇ ————————————

Not long ago, a friend contacted me because she needed prayer and spiritual counseling. I invited her over and she shared about the abuse she was suffering at the hands of her husband. I was both shocked and saddened for her and her family.

Just a couple of weeks prior, an online friend had asked me for prayer for her family. Her mentally ill husband had threatened suicide and said things that made her fear for herself and her children. She had to flee for their safety.

A few months back, I got to spend time with a friend whom I previously only knew online. She shared with me the abuse she had suffered at the hands of her ex-husband and her heart for those who now suffer abuse.

I have an accountability partner in writing and publishing. Her recently published book is a devotional for women who have been abused, offering Scripture, support, and encouragement. She writes from a place of experience.

All of these women shared these stories with me in about a six-month period, and I realized God was opening my eyes to something. These were all Christian women. They weren't walking around with a #metoo sign. They were either asking for prayer and spiritual guidance or using their story to help others.

I felt woefully unqualified and unprepared to help those who were seeking counsel.

So, I recently had the opportunity to attend a luncheon bringing awareness to the church about abusive relationships. Today I want to share with you some statistics and shed a little light on the subject of abuse, because it is far more common than I ever knew. We as Christian women need to be aware and know how we can get help or help someone else.

What is abuse?

> "Domestic violence (DV) (also called intimate partner violence (IPV), domestic abuse or relationship abuse) is a pattern of behaviors used by one partner to maintain power and control over another partner in an intimate relationship."[14]

I think it's important to remember that the abuse isn't always physical. Abusers specialize in emotional, mental, and verbal threats, often using manipulation, fear, and intimidation to control and confuse their victims.

One in three women in the United States is estimated to experience domestic abuse in her lifetime.[15] I wouldn't have believed that statistic until I started thinking about it. But in my family, my small group, and among my friends, that number bears out.

I am not a fan of the feminist movement; we have seen all too well in recent years how women have used the claim of abuse for manipulation and control, ruining the careers and families of innocent men.

But, as usual, Satan is really good at taking something real and hijacking it for his own purposes. As the body of Christ, we can't allow his deception to keep us from responding in support and love to those who are truly victims.

How should the church respond?

The luncheon I attended was designed to educate those in ministry about abusers, their victims, and how best to minister to them. Out of over 200 abused women their ministry had interviewed, most of them had experienced not being believed or being told to go back to their husbands and submit to them.

There are many reasons for this attitude. Some of it is misunderstanding of Scripture; some of it is unbelief because abusers are good at fooling others; and some of it is due to a lack of education and training for church staff.

I can't address all of these, and I don't claim to be an expert. What I can do is share the Word with you and some resources that can give you further understanding.

> "Submit to one another out of reverence for Christ. Wives, submit to your husbands as to the Lord. For the husband is the head of the wife as Christ is the head of the church, his body, of which he is the Savior. Now as the church submits to

Christ, so also wives should submit to their husbands in everything.

Husbands, love your wives, just as Christ loved the church and gave himself up for her to make her holy, cleansing her by the washing with water through the word, and to present her to himself as a radiant church without stain or wrinkle or any other blemish, but holy and blameless. In the same way, husbands ought to love their wives as their own bodies. He who loves his wife loves himself" (Ephesians 5:21-28).

This passage comes in the context of Paul's teaching on being filled with the Spirit. As we are filled with the Spirit, we come under God's control and live according to His Word (Ephesians 5:18-20). We should sing, give thanks, and submit to one another as a result.

This submission is mutual (submit to one another) and applies to all relationships, especially to the marriage relationship, as Paul then details. Wives are to submit to their husbands, which means "to yield one's own rights."[16]

What does submission look like?

Out of our submission to Christ as our Lord, we also submit to our husbands, yielding our rights. This is so important in a marriage. If Kenneth and I have a disagreement, then as long as he is following God, I will surrender my rights and follow his leadership. And I can do so because I trust the Lord.

But if you will notice, there is much more here about the husband's responsibility. A man who loves his wife to the point of sacrificing his own needs for hers is displaying a life "filled with the Spirit" and worthy of his wife's submission. This husband's loving care of his wife is always for her best.

In other words, our relationship in marriage should be a reflection of our relationship with Christ, who loved us and gave His life for us.

An abuser is selfish, self-centered, and self-serving. He will take these verses out of context in order to control his wife to do his bidding. He is usually jealous, angry, manipulative, and intimidating. Abusers aren't loving their wives with the love of Christ, therefore they are not reflecting God's love for the church in their relationship.

> "This is a profound mystery, but I am talking about Christ and the church. However, each one of you must love his wife as he loves himself, and the wife must respect her husband" (Ephesians 5:32-33).

Mutual love and respect. That's what Paul was talking about. Real love has been outlined for us in 1 Corinthians 13.

> "Love is patient, love is kind. It does not envy, it does not boast. It is not rude, it is not self-seeking, it is not easily angered, it keeps no record of wrongs. Love does not delight in evil but rejoices in truth. It always protects, always trusts, always hopes, always perseveres" (1 Corinthians 13:4-7).

There is hope.

The women I know who have been abused have some deep scars. Some of them are in counseling now. Some of them are still in battles with their spouses. Some of them are years removed from the abuse yet still get emotional when they recall the trauma of it.

But all of them are surviving with God's help. His heart is and always has been for the oppressed, the weak, and the needy. His heart is for you. If you or someone you know is suffering at the hands of an abuser, please seek help. If you are in ministry of any kind, inform yourself about the reality of abuse and how to respond to those in need.

And to my friends whose stories are shared here, you are loved immensely by the Father. He sees you. He hears you. He believes you. And He is for you.

WHEN LIFE DOESN'T GO THE WAY WE PLANNED: MARY, MOTHER OF JESUS

--------------------------------⟨∞⟩--------------------------------

Once upon a time in the land of Galilee, in a small town called Nazareth, there lived a young girl named Mary. She was beautiful with long, dark hair pulled back with a simple ribbon. In those days, when a girl reached her age, her father would begin to arrange her marriage to a young man from a good family.

Mary adored her father and believed that he knew her best and loved her most. She trusted him to choose the perfect mate for her. So one day, her father came home and announced that the betrothal meal would take place. The betrothal was a legally binding event that could only be broken by divorce.

Mary's father negotiated the bride price with the groom's family; after all, her home would lose a valuable daughter who contributed to their household. This payment demonstrated Mary's worth—that she was a treasure to her family.

On the day of the betrothal, a young man named Joseph set out to Mary's home, carrying with him the bride price, a gold ring, material for her dress, wine for the vow, and the ketubah or marriage contract.

When Mary opened the door, there stood Joseph—a handsome young man that she had known since childhood. She welcomed him in, butterflies churning in her stomach. The two of them shared a meal and drank the cup, which represented both joy and judgment—joy at the prospect of their new lives together and judgment should either of them ever be unfaithful.

They fed each other bread as a sign of their promise: Joseph promised to provide and protect; Mary promised to care and to comfort. Together they signed the ketubah, sealing their covenant to become man and wife.

Joseph placed a gold ring on the forefinger of her right hand, saying, "By this ring you are consecrated to me as my wife in accordance with the law of Moses and of Israel."

With excitement and anticipation, Joseph returned home to build an addition onto his family's house for him and his wife. Mary began sewing her wedding gown. When Joseph's work on their new home would be completed, he would return for his bride, and the wedding celebration would begin. They were now considered husband and wife, only awaiting the time when their marriage would be consummated, and they would become one.*

Their expectations soared as they anticipated building their new life together. And then...

> "In the sixth month, God sent the angel Gabriel to Nazareth, a town in Galilee, to a virgin pledged to be married to a man named Joseph, a descendant of David. The virgin's name was

Mary. The angel went to her and said, 'Greetings, you who are highly favored! The Lord is with you.'

Mary was greatly troubled at his words and wondered what kind of greeting this might be. But the angel said to her, 'Do not be afraid, Mary, you have found favor with God. You will be with child and give birth to a son, and you are to give him the name Jesus. He will be great and will be called the Son of the Most High. The Lord God will give him the throne of his father David, and he will reign over the house of Jacob forever; his kingdom will never end.'

'How will this be,' Mary asked the angel, 'since I am a virgin?'

The angel answered, 'The Holy Spirit will come upon you, and the power of the Most High will overshadow you. So the holy one to be born will be called the Son of God. Even Elizabeth your relative is going to have a child, and she who was said to be barren is in her sixth month. For nothing is impossible with God.'

'I am the Lord's servant,' Mary answered. 'May it be to me as you have said.' Then the angel left her" (Luke 1:26-38).

Talk about a change in plans! Mary had been making a dress and preparing for a wedding celebration. Now she was trying to figure out how to explain something she didn't understand herself. So, she prayed for courage and visited Joseph to tell him the news.

"Because Joseph her husband was a righteous man and did not want to expose her to public disgrace, he had in mind to divorce her quietly.

But after he had considered this, an angel of the Lord appeared to him in a dream and said, 'Joseph, son of David, do not be afraid to take Mary home as your wife, because what is conceived in her is from the Holy Spirit. She will give birth to a son, and you are to give him the name Jesus, because he will save his people from their sins'" (Matthew 1:19-21).

These two had been anticipating a great celebration with family and friends, and now they were facing an unexpected and unexplainable pregnancy. They had to deal with rumors, explanations to their parents, and the responsibility of bringing the Messiah into the world.

Mary didn't expect to travel 80 miles with a child in her womb or give birth in a cave with no family around. They probably didn't anticipate being on the run from Herod with no diapers, no pacifier, and (good grief!) no mama there to help her.

Their world was turned upside down.

Perhaps you have felt the sting of unmet expectations—the sudden loss of a loved one, some unexpected turn of events, a longing unfulfilled. Maybe you feel that your world has been turned upside down and you no longer anticipate with hope and joy.

Perhaps there are empty seats at your table this year, hurt feelings among family members, a lack of funds for gifts, or a sickness you are battling. You feel the pain and disappointment of all those unmet expectations.

The good news for you today is that we know the rest of Mary and Joseph's story. God is always true to His promises, and His promise of a Messiah who would save the world from sin was fulfilled through the unmet expectations of two teenagers.

Immanuel—God with us—slept in their very arms. God provided a manger to hold His Baby Boy, shepherds to welcome him into the world, and angels to sing His praise. God led them to Egypt and kept them safe. In the midst of their dashed hopes and unmet expectations, God showed up and used them to fulfill the greatest plan the world has ever known.

Their Christmas story became a story of redemption, peace, love, joy, and hope for all the world through Jesus. And their story brings hope to our story. Because we may face some dashed hopes and shattered dreams, but we can trust the God of Mary and Joseph to show up and work all things together for our good and His glory.

Immanuel will be with us, and He will bring comfort in our pain, peace in our troubles, His presence in our loneliness, His joy in our grief. He will take our pain and confusion and questions and disappointment and work them all together for our good and for His glory.

Will you trust God with your story? Will you trust that your Father loves you most and knows you best?

Because in the midst of your unmet expectations, a Savior has been born. He has come to heal the brokenhearted and to set the captives free. His name is Jesus, and He is here.

*The narrative is my own re-telling of the Christmas story. Much of the cultural context about Hebrew betrothal came from a teaching I heard by Judi Ebert.

ANXIETY, FRUSTRATION, AND CHRISTMAS: MARY, MOTHER OF JESUS

──────────── ⟨∽⟩ ────────────

Can you remember certain Christmas experiences you had as a child, the ones that gave you the goosebumps and made you feel all warm and snuggly and excited beyond belief? Do you have some special memories or traditions with your family growing up that you try to recreate with your family?

Or maybe your Christmases weren't all that great as a child, and you are desperate to create some memories worth having with your own children. Maybe you scroll through Facebook or Pinterest and want with all your heart to post the perfect Christmas family pictures—the ones with all the kids smiling around the perfect Christmas tree as Dad reads from Luke chapter 2.

I feel this way every year. I so want to make memories with my kids and feel the goosebumps and have a Christmas experience to remember that is 100% focused on Jesus. But somehow it seems that each year is filled with more anxiety than awe.

My family has been sick. So, I have been taking vitamins, sleeping on the couch, and desperately trying to not get sick myself. Yesterday was an all-morning doctor visit, lots of waiting in a germ-infested office, and my wondering if it would be rude to ask for a mask and gloves.

Then we spent more time waiting for prescriptions to be filled, so I thought I would tackle the grocery list while I waited. Of course, the list included foods for events that are coming and more gifts that I needed right away, but Kenneth was in the car miserable. Did I mention it POURED rain all day?

So, I hurriedly threw some essentials in the cart and raced back to the pharmacy at the time they said, only to have to wait some more. (It wasn't their fault. They had a gazillion prescriptions to fill.)

By then, my husband was texting for me to hurry, my daughter was texting for me to bring her some food, and I was feeling a ton of anxiety. Without everything on my list, I self-checked and left.

I stopped at KFC to get Bethany some comfort food and hurried home to unload the groceries, get some meds in Kenneth, and go to my desk to start working.

Only when we got home, Bethany's order from KFC did not include the mashed potatoes and gravy she asked for. So, I unloaded the groceries and jumped back in the car to return the individual side of corn and get my baby her comfort food.

By the time I got buckled in, I was feeling the stress and frustration begin to mount. It all just felt like too much. Does this sound familiar to anyone?

I bet it does to a young girl I wish I knew, one I would love to have coffee with and pick her brain with a thousand questions.

How long was your labor? How did you cut the cord? Did you pack those swaddling cloths before you left or find them in the cave? How long did it take for your milk to come in? Was it cold that night? Did you really put your baby in a feeding trough? Is that even sterile? Did anyone give y'all some light, blankets, anything? Did you want your mama?

Will you ever forget that night? Do you still get goosebumps? Did you feel the warmth and wonder and glory of Christmas? Did you ever think you would tell that story over and over and that you were making a wonderful, magical Christmas memory even though you were probably cold and miserable and in pain?

As I backed down the driveway yesterday, I turned the radio up and heard these words:

"A thrill of hope, the weary world rejoices."

And suddenly in that moment, the anxiety just melted away. As my voice sang out, my heart declared the desire to fall on my knees and hear the angel voices proclaiming:

"Glory to God in the highest, and on earth peace to men on whom his favor rests" (Luke 2:14).

I know many people who are really sick, grieving, struggling just to keep it together right now. They are dealing with loss, heartbreak, financial difficulties, and pain. They aren't too concerned with having a perfect holiday experience. They just want to make it through the day.

And yet many of them are at peace because they know the Prince of Peace. That's the glory of Christmas!

Christmas isn't about seeking perfectly memorable experiences. It's not about Pinterest projects and to-do lists. Christmas is about the hope, peace, love, and joy that Jesus brings. It's about Emmanuel—God with us, bringing the very presence of God into our lives so that we can know Him personally. Christmas is God coming to dwell with us so that we can forever dwell with Him.

This Christmas, instead of trying to make a magical memory, let's bow in God's presence and meditate on the wonder of the Word made flesh. Instead of stressing over all that needs to be done, let's take time to reach out to someone who is hurting.

Let's stop trying to create a warm, fuzzy experience and just be thankful that we can experience the mercy and grace of the King who has set us free. We don't know what the future holds, but we celebrate the One who does, and in that knowledge we can have peace.

My house is still a mess, littered with used Kleenex and prescription bottles. I still don't have everything I need for gifting and baking. But that's okay. My Savior came into the world in a less than favorable environment to a young girl who was just willing to say yes, and that was the most magical, goosebump-making, picture-perfect moment in all of history.

> "And Mary said, "Behold, I am the servant of the Lord; let it be to me according to your word" (Luke 1:38, ESV).

Let's take a cue from Mary and just bow a knee at the manger. Because sometimes the quiet, ordinary moments can make the best memories after all.

LIVING A LIFE
OF DEVOTION:
ANNA

It was a divine moment in time—one of those fleeting opportunities to experience glory. And one woman was ready. She isn't remembered all that much in the Christmas story, but she was there—faithfully serving, hoping, and waiting.

At Christmastime we hear about the angels who announced Jesus' birth. We remember the shepherds who ran back and told everyone the Messiah had been born.

We especially recall the obedience and faith of a young couple, Mary and Joseph, who sacrificed their reputation and plans for the future in order to obey the call of God on their lives. But we rarely hear the story of Anna, a prophetess who recognized the divine gift of the Baby and shared that news with others.

Married for only seven years and widowed until she was eighty-four, Anna was a devoted woman of God who spent her life seeking and serving her God.

> "There was also a prophetess, Anna, the daughter of Phanuel, of the tribe of Asher. She was very old; she had lived with her

husband seven years after her marriage, and then was a widow until she was eighty-four. She never left the temple but worshiped night and day, fasting and praying" (Luke 2:36-37).

When Mary and Joseph showed up at the temple to present their firstborn and dedicate Him to the Lord according to the Law, Anna was ready and waiting to experience His presence and to proclaim the news.

> "Coming up to them at that very moment, she gave thanks to God and spoke about the child to all who were looking forward to the redemption of Jerusalem" (Luke 2:38).

Anna could have missed this moment in time, but because of her devotion to God, she was privileged to experience the most spectacular event in human history—God becoming a man to save us.

Anna's example teaches us five ways we can live a life of devotion to God.

First, Anna was a prophetess. She used the gifts God gave her to serve Him faithfully. Anna didn't use loss or age as excuses. She devoted her life to serving God no matter what.

Second, she stayed in the presence of God. Historians have noted that Herod's temple was very large and included many rooms, including places that Anna may have been allowed to live in.

We don't really know the details of why she stayed at the temple, but we do know that the temple was the only place for the Jews where God's presence dwelt. For her, being close to God was how she determined to live out her years.

Third, Anna worshiped day and night with prayer and fasting. Worship is an attitude of the heart. As Anna went about the duties of the temple, her heart was always in tune with God through prayer and through fasting.

Fourth, Anna thanked God for the gift of His Son. She knew the significance of the Baby being dedicated to God that day. She knew the salvation of all mankind was before her, something she had waited for all her life. And her heart was thankful that God had fulfilled His promise.

Last, she proclaimed the news of what God had done. The glory had returned to the temple! She proclaimed that the Redeemer promised through the prophet Isaiah had come at last. It wasn't news her little 84-year-old body could keep to herself.

What if we lived like Anna? What if we resolved that from here on out, we are going to live our lives as if nothing else mattered but Jesus? What would that look like for you and me?

Can we devote ourselves to use the gifts God has given us to serve Him—no excuses? Can we abide in His presence, even as we work and love and care for those around us?

Do you think we can let a heart of worship be our lifestyle, our spirits connecting with God's, our desire for more of Him outweighing our concern for ourselves? Would we be willing to fast and pray for more of God in our lives?

Can we live each moment with gratitude, even when there is loss and pain in the midst of it?

And do we dare to proclaim to all those in need of redemption that the Savior has come? It's not just a cute Christmas story. It's the truth of all human existence and for all eternity.

We will fail. We will be tested and challenged. But I would rather seek to live a life of devotion to God even in my failures, than to continue to live with any less than all He died to give us.

> "But whatever was to my profit I now consider loss for the sake of Christ. What is more, I consider everything a loss compared to the surpassing greatness of knowing Christ Jesus my Lord, for whose sake I have lost all things. I consider them rubbish, that I may gain Christ and be found in him, not having a righteousness that comes from the law, but that which is through faith in Christ—the righteousness that comes from God and is by faith" (Philippians 3:7-9).

How about you? Do you want to live a life of devotion to God? The decision to pursue God with all your heart will be a defining moment in time.

Don't miss it.

HOW TO HAVE NEW LIFE

Do you want to know how to have new life?

We were each created by God to know and worship Him. God loves you and desires a personal relationship with you.

The Bible teaches us that we are all sinners. Romans 3:23 says, "for all have sinned and fall short of the glory of God." God is holy and righteous and good. He created the world and all that is in it. But we are all born with a sinful nature because He made us with a free will—the opportunity to choose whether or not we will follow Him. Left to ourselves, we will fall short of His glory and righteousness. This sin separates us from God and leads only to death. Romans 6:23 says, "for the wages of sin is death."

Because God loves us so much, He made a way for us to know Him through His Son. "But God demonstrates his own love for us in this: while we were still sinners, Christ died for us" (Romans 5:8). God sent His only Son, Jesus, who lived a perfect life, to die on the cross for us as payment for our sin. He took the punishment on Himself so that we could be free from sin's penalty.

The rest of Romans 6:23 (above) says this: "but the gift of God is eternal life in Christ Jesus." We are sinners, and yet through Jesus and the gift of God, we can have eternal life. The truth is that we really can have a personal relationship with God through His Son, Jesus.

So, what do you do to be saved?

Romans 10:9-10 tells us "That if you confess with your mouth, 'Jesus is Lord,' and believe in your heart that God raised him from the dead, you will be saved. For it is with your heart that you believe and are justified, and it is with your mouth that you confess and are saved."

If God is speaking to your heart right now and you want to be saved, pray a prayer like this one:

Lord God,

I believe that You are God and that You created me to know You. I believe that You sent your Son to die on the cross for my sins and that He rose again and lives forever. I know that I am a sinner and I confess my sins to You now. I ask You to forgive me and cleanse me and come to live inside my heart and be the Lord of my life. I choose to follow You and live for You from this day forward.

In Jesus' name,

Amen

If you just prayed a prayer like this one, please let me know the good news. Find a Bible-believing Christian church and begin to read the Bible and talk to God every day. You've just begun your new life in Him. Congratulations! Your life will never be the same!

ACKNOWLEDGMENTS

As I wrap up my fifth book, I'm really at a loss for words to express how blessed and humbled I feel to even be doing this. So many women out there are much more qualified and far better writers than I. But God called me out and set me on this journey, opening one door after another. I just keep following Him to the next thing, wondering when this writing business will end, and I'll go back to being a classroom teacher. But so far, this is where God keeps leading me.

So, to the Lord, who for now keeps this door open, thank You for allowing me to be on this adventure with You. You have the Words of life. Where else would I go?

To Kenneth, Josiah & Moriah, and Bethany, you are the best part of me. Thank you for your love, laughter, encouragement, and presence in my life. I love you more than anything but Jesus.

To Mema, you're still the best. No other words needed.

To Michelle, whose wisdom shows up quite a bit in this book, thank you for being the right kind of friend—faithful and true.

To Heather, your help, support, prayers, and encouragement have taken this ministry to another level. I can't thank you enough for talking me through the struggles.

To my small group, you are an invaluable part of my life. Thank you for real community, love, discipleship, and accountability.

To all the women of *Growing Your Faith*, you are more to me than a Facebook group. I love and pray for each of you and truly want God's best for your life. Keep seeking Him first.

And to every woman out there who has ever felt rejected, betrayed, abandoned, mistreated, ashamed, confused, defeated, or without hope, this one's for you. You don't have to do more, be better, or measure up. You just need Jesus.

ABOUT THE AUTHOR

Jennifer Hayes Yates is a wife, mama, writer, and speaker with an empty nest and a Southern accent. Having taught in Christian education for twenty-two years, she has a passion for communicating God's truth and inspiring others to seek Him.

Jennifer is now a blogger, best-selling author, and passionate speaker. She serves in her church as a Sunday school teacher and music director and leads a small group of awesome ladies in Bible study at her home.

Lover of all things Jesus, books, and coffee, she can be found in quiet corners or busy spaces, sipping lattes, studying commentaries, and chatting up strangers.

Jennifer has now published four best sellers: *Seek Him First: How to Hear from God, Walk in His Will, and Change Your World; Let's Run: Running the Race with Faith and Perseverance; Inside Out and Upside Down:*

How Intimacy with Jesus Changes Everything, and her latest book *Drawing Ever Closer: 365 Days of Transforming Truth.*

But she's still just a small-town girl hoping to glorify God in all she writes and make a few disciples along the way.

You can follow Jennifer on Facebook, Instagram, and at Jenniferhyates.com.

NOTE FROM THE AUTHOR

Thank you for reading *Just Like Us*!

My heart is for you to get to know Jesus better, for you to know who you are in Him, and for you to grow in your faith walk. I pray this book has been a catalyst for that end.

I would love to get your feedback. If *Just Like Us* has been a blessing to you, would you consider leaving a helpful review on Amazon? It would mean so much to me and help me as I plan future books.

Thank you and may God bless you as you grow in Him.

Jennifer

MORE BY
JENNIFER HAYES YATES

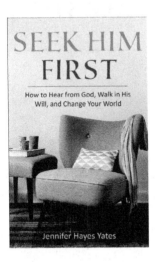

Do you struggle to have a consistent quiet time with God?

Do you wonder how to know if you are hearing from God?

Do you desire to know God's will for your life?

Do you want to make a difference for the kingdom of God?

Seek Him First has been written to show you exactly how you can seek God and find the direction you need for the journey. This book is for those who know God has a plan for their lives, but don't know how to make it a reality from day to day.

- Develop a consistent daily quiet time with God.
- Learn how to know when God is speaking to you and follow His plan for your life.
- Explore different strategies for Bible study.
- Discover ways to feed your soul and be satisfied.
- Get on mission with the God of the universe and change your world.

RUNNING THE RACE WITH FAITH AND PERSEVERANCE

A 6-week Bible Study with Weekend Devotions

JENNIFER HAYES YATES

Every race is a challenge.

Hills, valleys, dips, and curves; pain, thirst, weariness, and overwhelm—sometimes it's just easier to take a seat on the sideline and slip off our running shoes.

But God has inspired us in His Word to run the race with faith and perseverance and to finish well. He gives us examples of others who faced some of the same challenges, yet remained faithful.

Let's Run! explores the faith chapter of Hebrews by taking us back to the Old Testament and the stories of some ordinary people who faced enormous challenges but managed to stay in the race. This Bible study will give you not only a look at their lives, but also an opportunity to apply the same principles of faith to your own life, to keep you in the race and running toward the prize.

- Discover how worship and the Word can help your faith grow.
- Learn how to apply these principles in your own life, family, and church.
- Develop a strategy for handling challenges to your faith.
- Gain a new perspective on church and ministry.

Let's Run! is a 6-week Bible study which includes weekend devotions to recap the principles learned each week, as well as ideas for group study. Join Jennifer and be inspired to lace up and get back in the race!

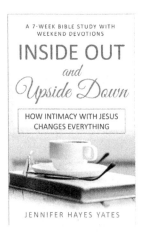

Do you feel there should be more to the Christian life?

Are you hungry for more of God?

Do you struggle to live out a faith that is counter-cultural to the world around you?

Inside Out and Upside Down: How Intimacy with Jesus Changes Everything is a 7-week Bible study that explores the Gospels and the Song of Solomon to help you discover God's plan for personal relationship and kingdom living. In these weeks of study, you will

- Understand the difference between religion and relationship.
- Learn how to find satisfaction in Christ alone.
- Discover God's purpose for community through the local church.
- Explore the counter-cultural kingdom of God.
- Assess the costs and the benefits of kingdom living.

Each week of Bible study ends with a Weekend Devo to summarize the lessons and give opportunity for thoughtful reflection and application. Dig into this study and discover a life of intimacy and adventure with the King that supersedes religion and inspires devotion.

Drawing Ever Closer is a daily devotional for women based on the books of Job, Psalms, Proverbs, Ecclesiastes, and Song of Songs.

- In these devotions you will
- Discover the heart of worship.
- Learn how to walk in wisdom.
- Understand your purpose in life.
- Explore love and passion.
- Gain a godly perspective on pain.

Start your day in the transforming truth to be gleaned in these poetic books, and let His truth establish in you a firm foundation of worship, wisdom, purpose, passion, and a godly response to pain.

"Send forth your light and your truth, let them guide me; let them bring me to your holy mountain, to the place where you dwell" (Psalm 43:3).

ENDNOTES

1 https://www.lexico.com/en/definition/favoritism (accessed January 21, 2020).

2 Kenneth Barker, *The NIV Study Bible*, (Grand Rapids: Zondervan, 1973, 1978, 1984), 46.

3 Barker, 1536.

4 https://abcnews.go.com/Entertainment/captain-marvel-star-brie-larson-reveals-iconic-role/story?id=61458900 (accessed January 23, 2020).

5 https://jewsforjesus.org/publications/newsletter/newsletter-jun-1988/jesus-and-the-role-of-women/ (accessed January 21, 2020).

6 Charles F. Pfeiffer and Everett F. Harrison, Eds., *The Wycliffe Bible Commentary*, (Nashville: The Southwestern Company, 1962), 1090.

7 John R. Kohlenberger, Ed., *NIV Exhaustive Bible Concordance*, Third Edition (Grand Rapids: Zondervan, 1990, 1999, 2015), 1473.

8 Kohlenberger, 1505.

9 Gary Smalley and John Trent, Ph.D, *Giving the Blessing* (Nashville, TN: Thomas Nelson Publishers, 1993, January 5).

10 D.A. Carson, *Praying with Paul: A Call to Spiritual Reformation*, (Grand Rapids: Baker Publishing Group, 1992, 2014), 165.

11 Kohlenberger, 1544.

12 Ibid, 1545.

13 Ibid, 1507.

14 https://www.thehotline.org/is-this-abuse/abuse-defined/ (accessed January 21, 2020).

15 https://www.calledtopeace.org/ (accessed January 21, 2020).

16 Barker, 1798.

Made in the USA
Columbia, SC
30 March 2020